VILLAGES OF EDINBURGH:
AN ILLUSTRATED GUIDE

VILLAGES OF EDINBURGH:

AN ILLUSTRATED GUIDE

Volume 1

Malcolm Cant

Modern photography by Jenni Wood

Maps by Bryan Ryalls

Foreword by

Sir Tom Farmer C.B.E., K.C.S.G.

MALCOLM CANT PUBLICATIONS

First published in 1997 by
Malcolm Cant Publications
13 Greenbank Row Edinburgh EH10 5SY
Reprinted in 2001

Text copyright © Malcolm Cant
Photographs, as acknowledged, are the copyright of Jenni Wood
Maps are the copyright of Bryan Ryalls

ISBN 0 9526099 1 6

British Library Cataloguing-in-Publication Data
A catalogue record for this book is available on request

Typeset and originated by Carnegie Publishing Ltd
Carnegie House, Chatsworth Road, Lancaster LA1 4SL
Printed and bound in Great Britain by Cromwell Press,
Trowbridge, Wiltshire

To

my first grandchild

Joanna

who weighs me up and weighs me down

Contents

Foreword

People often tell me that Kwik-Fit is a big organisation, and I suppose it is. I don't see it that way. Kwik-Fit is made up of lots of small communities, all living their own lives, delighting their customers, relating to and interacting with their own communities. Certainly, I want them to be proud of Kwik-Fit, but most of all, I want them to be proud of their own centre and of the service they are providing to the community.

I come from one of these small local communities. In my childhood, Leith was my world. Edinburgh was a big place up the road. Today the distinction has blurred. Tomorrow, unless we protect its identity, Leith could become little more than a name for an area.

Like Leith, other Edinburgh villages such as Cramond, Davidson's Mains, Newhaven, Corstorphine, Barnton must not just become place names on a map and memories in the minds of the older generation. In recording their identities, Malcolm Cant has not just preserved an endangered part of Edinburgh's – and Scotland's – history, he has performed a valuable public service. The fact that the story of Edinburgh's villages also happens to be such a fascinating one is simply the icing on the cake.

That is why I am delighted to give my wholehearted endorsement to this book on the villages of Edinburgh. It helps to put a focus on local communities and on the importance of keeping their individual characteristics alive. It reminds us of that nowadays often elusive human trait called character. And it teaches us that facing the future does not mean forgetting the past.

The book is written in a style to encourage readers to walk the route and actually visit the many places of interest. With that in mind, an excellent map of each village, drawn by Bryan Ryalls, has been included at the beginning of each chapter. The text is greatly enhanced by a wide variety of photographs, which include the work of Jenni Wood.

Sir Tom Farmer C.B.E., K.C.S.G.

Acknowledgments

I am indebted to a wide range of people for their assistance in bringing this volume to fruition. They include the staff of: the Edinburgh City Archaeologist's Department; the Edinburgh City Archivist's Department; Edinburgh University Library; the Edinburgh Room of the Central Library; Historic Scotland; the National Library of Scotland; the Royal Commission on the Ancient and Historical Monuments of Scotland; and The Scotsman Publications Ltd.

In particular areas I derived a lot of help and encouragement from the various local societies and people interested in local history:

CORSTORPHINE: Corstorphine Primary School; Corstorphine Trust; Andrew B. Eadie; the Edinburgh Tapestry Co. Ltd.

CRAMOND: the City Archaeologist; Cramond Heritage Trust; Eric Jamieson.

DAVIDSON'S MAINS: Robert Brown; Rev. Mary F. Harrison; Miss E. M. Smith; Mrs C. Veitch.

DEAN: Drumsheugh Baths Club; Miss Dorothy L. Forrester; Scottish Episcopal Church; Yeoman McAllister, Architects.

DUDDINGSTON: Holy Rood High School; Mrs April Johnson-Marshall; Percy Johnson Marshall & Partners, Architects; Colin McLean; Mrs Susan Mercer; Charles Rawcliffe; Scottish Wildlife Trust, Lothian Branch; Sheep Heid Inn.

NEWHAVEN: Huntly House Museum; Newhaven Heritage Museum; Peacock Inn; Harry Ramsden's.

RESTALRIG: Mrs Norma Armstrong; Alistair R. Cockburn; Mr & Mrs Hurley; Charles Arthur Kemp.

STOCKBRIDGE: Donaldson's College; Rev. A. Ian Dunlop; the Edinburgh Academy; Rose Pipes; St Stephen's Centre; Stockbridge Parish Church; Stockbridge Primary School; Theatre Workshop.

I am also indebted to Jenni Wood for the excellent modern photography, and to Bryan Ryalls, assisted by Mairi Grant, for the clear and informative maps of the various locations. Additional photographs are acknowledged throughout the text. John and Val Tuckwell undertook the editorial work, checked the proofs and compiled the index: Neville Moir then steered the whole project through the design and printing stages to the finished book.

I would also like to thank Sir Tom Farmer C.B.E., K.C.S.G. for writing the Foreword and for his unassuming hospitality on each occasion that we met.

Finally, I thank my wife, Phyllis, and our family who were always on hand for a host of tasks associated with the book.

Malcolm Cant

Introduction

It is more than a decade since I first made a study of some of the surviving village communities in Edinburgh. The result of that research was published for me by John Donald Publishers Ltd., of Edinburgh in two volumes as *Villages of Edinburgh*, which are now out of print. Recently I looked through my research notes again and revisited the places which had occupied so much of my time a decade earlier. I discovered that time had not, in fact, stood still and that important changes had taken place. When I contacted the various local societies and history groups I was very favourably impressed by the amount of work which had been undertaken in gathering slides and prints, and recording the history of their own locality. Much more information had come to light since I was last involved, and much more still lies beneath the surface. In January 1997 Edinburgh's City Archaeologist announced a discovery of international importance at Cramond, where the local ferryman, Robert Graham, spotted a statue of a lioness, sticking out of the mudbanks of the River Almond. The stone relic has been dated to the Roman occupation of Cramond more than 1500 years ago.

After studying all the villages again I decided to update my information and alter my style to present *Villages of Edinburgh: an illustrated guide*. In doing this I hope to encourage my readers, not only to enjoy the book at home, but to visit these village communities and actually walk the route. With that in mind I have arranged the script topographically, supported by a much wider selection of photographs (including aerial views) depicting the main places of local interest. A detailed street map, with the relevant places marked, has also been included at the beginning of each chapter. In addition, a general map of Edinburgh appears at the beginning of the book showing the location of the villages included in each volume. All the villages can be reached by car, but in this enlightened age my recommendation is to use public transport: looking at the view from the top deck of a bus is infinitely more varied than looking at the back of the car in front.

In the first volume I have concentrated on the villages in what might be described as the northern hemisphere of the city, which includes

Corstorphine, Cramond, Davidson's Mains, Dean, Duddingston, Newhaven, Restalrig and Stockbridge. The second volume will deal with the villages on the south side, namely Colinton, Gilmerton, Juniper Green, Liberton, Longstone, Morningside, Slateford and Swanston.

Malcolm Cant

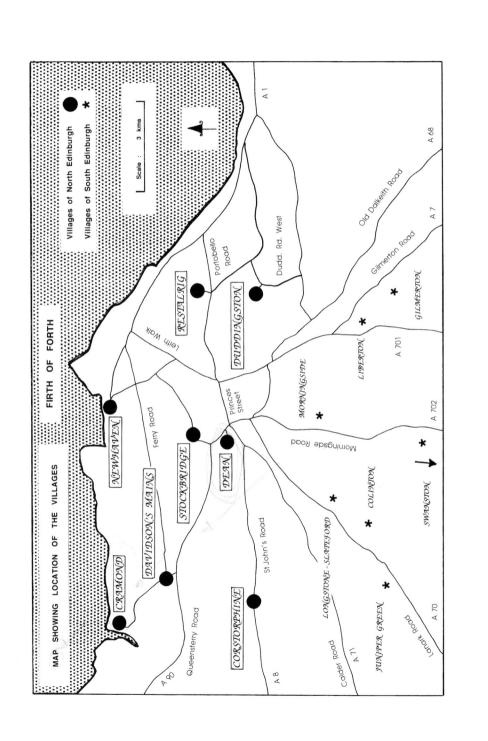

MAP SHOWING LOCATION OF THE VILLAGES

FIRTH OF FORTH

Villages of North Edinburgh ●
Villages of South Edinburgh ✳

Scale : 3 kms

CRAMOND

NEWHAVEN

DAVIDSON'S MAINS

STOCKBRIDGE

DEAN

RESTALRIG

DUDDINGSTON

MORNINGSIDE

LIBERTON

GILMERTON

COLINTON

SWANSTON

JUNIPER GREEN

CORSTORPHINE

Ferry Road

Queensferry Road

A 90

St John's Road

A 8

Calder Road

A 71

Longstone - Slateford

Lanark Road

A 70

Morningside Road

A 702

A 701

A 7

Gilmerton Road

Old Dalkeith Road

A 68

A 1

Princes Street

Leith Walk

Portobello Road

Dudd. Rd. West

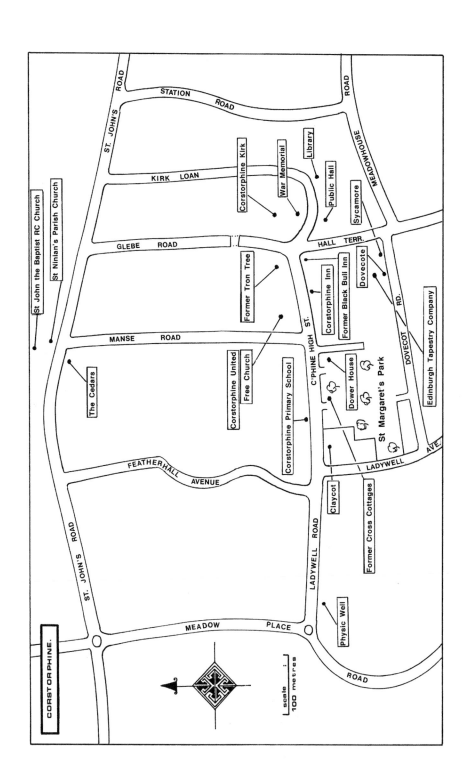

CHAPTER ONE

Corstorphine

The 'old' village of Corstorphine lies approximately three miles directly west of Princes Street, reached by way of Haymarket and Murrayfield. There were really two villages, each of which retains its own character: the old village lies a few hundred yards to the south of the present main road, and the new village grew up along the line of St John's Road, which became the main route out of Edinburgh to Glasgow. The historic centre of Corstorphine is undoubtedly the old village, originally only a cluster of houses to the east of the narrow isthmus separating Gogar Loch from Corstorphine Loch. Gogar Loch was by far the smaller of the two, extending westward from the village, for a distance of approximately a mile and three-quarters, over the district of South Gyle. Corstorphine Loch, on the other hand, extended eastwards in a long narrow plain before widening out to cover the present districts of Balgreen and Roseburn. On the strategically important strip of land between the two lochs, the ancient family of Forrester built the impregnable defence, Corstorphine Castle, in the late fourteenth century. The old village remained close to the protection of the castle for several centuries, and it was not until the mid-nineteenth century that the new village developed to the north. During the twentieth century the name Corstorphine has been applied to an ever-expanding suburb stretching from Saughtonhall westwards to the city boundary.

The derivation of the name Corstorphine is uncertain. There are several suggestions, however, one of which is that it was the crossing place from the River Forth over the hill used by a Norse warrier called Thorfinn.

This aerial view of Corstorphine Old Parish Church, in 1980, shows clearly the unusual roof construction of the kirk, surrounded by its ancient graveyard. To the right, the grassed area was known as Irish Corner until the cottages were demolished c. 1928.
Crown Copyright: Royal Commission on the Ancient and Historical Monuments of Scotland.

THE OLD VILLAGE

Corstorphine Old Parish Kirk, or the Parish Church of St John the Baptist, in Kirk Loan, is the obvious starting point for a walking tour of the old village. Its stone roof and irregular roofline mark it out as Corstorphine's most distinctive building, parts of which date from the beginning of the fifteenth century. Its long and eventful history prompted D. M. Thomson, in 1946, to observe in *The Corstorphine Heirloom* that 'it bears the marks of having been more than once rudely handled in times of national crisis, although the finger of time has smoothed out most of the scars'. The first definite record of a church on this site is of the parish church of St Mary in a charter of David I dated 1128. The church survived until 1646 when it was absorbed into the north aisle of St John's. The present church of St John began as a very modest chapel built in 1404 in fulfilment of a vow by Sir Adam Forrester, and later used as a place of burial for himself and his family. After his death in 1405 Sir Adam's son John installed two choir boys and increased the number of chaplains to five. This was the basis of the collegiate church in 1429 but it was not until 1436 that its status was confirmed by Pope Eugenius. It was the first Sir John Forrester who was responsible for the early additions to the church, many of them initiated before collegiate status had been granted. The fifteenth-century church, which incorporated the votive chapel, consisted of the present chancel and vestry, nave, bell tower and south transept, and probably a matching north transept. In 1646 the adjacent parish church of St Mary was demolished to allow the construction of the north aisle and extension of the north transept, along with a porch attached to the west of the bell tower constructed from stones taken from the ruins of St Mary's. In the early eighteenth century a gallery was built with access from an outside stair, the cost being met by Sir Andrew Myrtoun of Gogar House. Extensive reorganisation of the interior of the church was done by William Burn, the architect, in 1828, much of which was 'corrected' by George Henderson in 1905. The distinctive square tower has finials on each corner of the wallhead, and the squat stone steeple is divided into three tiers. The bell has an interesting inscription:

SIR JAMES FORRESTER GIFTED ME TO THIS KIRK
ANNO 1577 AND THE HERETORS OF CORSTORPHINE
ME RENEUED ANNO 1728 R.M. FECIT EDR.

Corstorphine Old Parish Church in its modern setting.
Courtesy of W. G. Dey.

R.M. of Edinburgh may refer to either Robert Meikle or Robert Maxwell, both of whom were well known bell founders. On the east gable of the church (nearest to Kirk Loan) there is an equally interesting feature. It is the beacon light niche dating from 1429 and kept in regular use until 1769. In the days when the ground around Corstorphine was covered by the loch and marshland, it had become the duty of the priests to raise a burning lamp on a pulley into the niche to give direction to anyone travelling by land or by water. The cost of maintaining this service was financed by the endowment of 'the lamp acre', a piece of ground near Coltbridge, now commemorated in Lampacre Road in Corstorphine. In 1958 the Corstorphine Rotary Club gifted and installed a modern electric lamp in the niche as a reminder of this ancient practice. The interior of the church is also famous for the recumbent effigies of the Forrester family, notably of the first Sir John Forrester and his wife, on the left of the vestry door, and their son, the second Sir John Forrester, on the right of the vestry door.

The interior of Corstorphine Old Parish Church showing the pulpit and the recumbent effigy of Adam Forrester on the right.
Courtesy of the Corstorphine Trust.

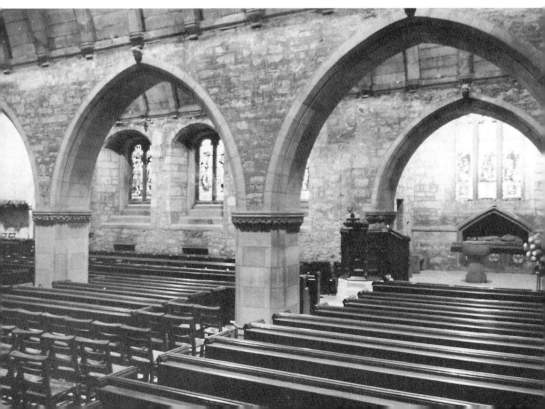

In Corstorphine Kirkyard this ancient tomb, with a wealth of detail on its reverse side, was erected to Janet Muirhead, daughter of Alexander Muirhead, Portioner in Corstorphine, who died on 28th December 1751, aged seventeen years. *Photograph by Jenni Wood.*

The Forrester family name is synonymous with that of Corstorphine. Prior to 1376 Adam Forrester lived in Forrester's Wynd on the south side of the High Street, near the present George IV Bridge. He was a man of ability and ambition who became Lord Provost of Edinburgh, and later Deputy-Governor of Edinburgh Castle. His first involvement in Corstorphine was in 1374 when he acquired the lands of Corstorphine from William More, and built Corstorphine Castle as the seat of the Forrester family. When George, the tenth head of the Forrester family, was created a peer in 1633, he took the title Lord Forrester of Corstorphine, but little did he know that his elevation was to prove a turning point in the history of the family. Although he had five daughters, his only son had predeceased him without issue, and he therefore decided to resolve the matter of his succession during his own lifetime. Tempted by the natural desire to maintain the family house and name, George made the fatal mistake of favouring one child at the expense of the others. He relinquished his title, and handed the barony to James Baillie, the husband of Joanna his fourth daughter. On the death of George, in 1654, James Baillie became the second Lord Forrester of Corstorphine, but he was not equal to the task. He neglected the estates; he incurred heavy debts; he drank too much and too often at the Black Bull Inn in the old village; and he engaged in extramarital relationships, principally with Christian Nimmo, his first wife's niece. From the seeds of debauchery he was later to reap a dismal harvest. His first wife Joanna died very young, as did William their only child. When his second wife Janet Ruthven also died he lost all purpose in life. During one of his bouts of drinking he supposedly doubted the morality of Christian Nimmo with whom he had been associating. When she heard the gossip she came to Corstorphine Castle on the night of 26th August 1679, only to be told that James was still at the Black Bull Inn. When they eventually met up at the famous Corstorphine Sycamore tree there was a violent quarrel during which James repeated his accusations. Incensed by the slur on her character and smarting from his refusal to marry her, Christian drew the sword from his scabbard and ran the blade through her drunken paramour. Leaving Lord Forrester dead, she fled but was later captured and was executed in Edinburgh on 12th November 1679. On the death of James the second Lord Forrester, so great was the trauma that his brother, heir to the estate, did not take the title of third Lord Forrester. The

The Black Bull Inn, High Street *c*. 1899, where James, the second Lord Forrester, took courage before his fateful encounter with Christian Nimmo at the Sycamore Tree in 1679. The Oakland plaque was added in 1904.
Courtesy of the Corstorphine Trust.

estate became burdened with debts and was sold in 1698 to Hugh Wallace W.S. of Ingliston, and then, in 1713, to Sir James Dick of Prestonfield, in whose family it remained for the next century and a half.

One might wonder what tangible evidence remains in the old village to link it with these stirring moments in history. The answer, surprisingly, is more than might have been expected, although naturally the links are interspersed with the more mundane aspects of village life. Leaving the Kirk and proceeding south on Kirk Loan we come to Corstorphine Public Library, built in 1927 on the site of Paddockholm Cottage. Prior to this, the library was housed in the eastmost section of the turreted red sandstone building, Corstorphine Public Hall. The main section to the west, with the twin turrets, is the original Public Hall built in 1891. Above the doorway there is a most interesting pediment containing the Forrester hunting horn in the tympanum, and the Scottish thistle on the apex, flanked by two clinging reptiles. The significance, if any, of the reptiles to Corstorphine, is not known. The former library section has a similar doorway except that the tympanum contains an open book. The area around the War Memorial at the junction of Kirk Loan and Saughton Road North was formerly Irish Corner, named after a cluster of small cottages inhabited by Irish labourers who had worked on the Edinburgh-Glasgow Railway, the Caledonian Railway and the Union Canal. Nearby, in Hall Terrace, only two of the row of single-storey cottages now remain. They do, however, help to consolidate the historical importance of this corner which includes the former Black Bull Inn at which Lord Forrester took courage before his fateful encounter with Christian Nimmo. At the beginning of the twentieth century the building was renovated and a stone plaque was added on the projecting east gable, 'Ye Olde Inne Oakland 1904'. The embellishments also appear to contain the date 1561 and the initials CDB, for Christopher Douglas Brown who funded the restoration.

South of Hall Terrace at the east end of Dovecot Road is living proof of the murder of Lord Forrester – the Corstorphine Sycamore – completely dominating the corner when it is in full foliage. The tree, which gives its name to the species *Acer Pseudoplatanus Corstorphinense*, is protected by a Preservation Order of 1955, and in 1970 was gifted to the Corstorphine Trust with a small piece of ground round the tree. Inevitably its great antiquity has given rise to some imaginative stories. On moonlight nights the ghost of Christian Nimmo is said to appear holding a bloody sword in her hand and moaning and wailing beneath the branches of the old sycamore. G. Upton Selway, writing in 1890, also relates the legend that Lord Forrester is supposed to have buried treasure beneath the tree and that at least one villager was frightened off by hearing a voice from beneath the tree commanding him to stop digging – a legend perhaps, but still a warning to anyone tempted to excavate too near its hallowed roots. A short distance to the west of the sycamore is the sixteenth-century Corstorphine Dovecot, its great bulk rising high above the boundary wall of the Dovecot studios. Like many similar dovecots, its preservation probably owes much to the old Scottish superstition that destruction of a dovecot meant death, within a year, of the lady of the house. Many Scottish dovecots are

The Corstorphine Dovecot, photographed in 1950, on the north side of Dovecot Road, dates from the sixteenth century. It has twenty-eight tiers providing 1060 nesting boxes. To its right is the famous Corstorphine Sycamore, believed to be over 500 years old. *Courtesy of the Corstorphine Trust.*

rectangular in shape, but the Corstorphine Dovecot, like that at Lochend, is circular. It is divided horizontally by three string courses and has six entrance holes in the south wall, above the middle course. The walls are about four feet thick at the base, with twenty-eight tiers providing 1060 stone nesting boxes. The entrance is on the north side, the door being embellished by ornamental ironwork.

The Corstorphine Dovecot stands in the garden of the Edinburgh Tapestry Company which was founded as the Dovecot Studios in 1912 in Dovecot Road. The dovecot was the insignia woven into each tapestry in the early days of the studio: it was later changed to a flying dove but in recent years has reverted to the original dovecot. The studio was founded by the fourth Marquess of Bute, with the first two master weavers, Gordon Berry and John Glassbrook, coming from William Morris's famous studio at Merton Abbey. The large, historical and finely woven tapestries of this era were destined for the walls of the many Bute family homes. The Company closed for the duration of the

Weavers drawing the cartoon, by the artist Skeoch Cumming, for the Prince of the Gael tapestry *c.*1935. The unfinished tapestry, commissioned by the fifth Marquess of Bute, is still on the loom at the Dovecot Studios in Corstorphine. *Courtesy of the Edinburgh Tapestry Company Limited.*

Second World War as all the weavers had enlisted. When it reopened, the members of the Bute family decided on a change of emphasis from large tapestries to smaller panels designed by well-known artists, intended for sale, and now the studio is mainly a commercial venture concentrating on commissioned work. In 1980 the studio had a major retrospective exhibition entitled 'Master Weavers' during the Edinburgh International Festival. The studio's work is known around the world, and it has translated the work of the best-known British and American artists into tapestry. In 1995 twenty-four tapestries from the

The ancient Forrester lintel stone, photographed here at The Cedars, Manse Road in 1954, commemorates the marriage of Henry Forrester and Helenor Preston of Craigmillar in the late sixteenth century.
Courtesy of the Corstorphine Trust.

Dovecot Studios were exhibited in the Rotunda Building in Hong Kong, and in 1996 the Studios began the largest tapestry ever to have been woven in the United Kingdom. It measures seven metres square and has been commissioned by the new British Library at St Pancras, in London.

Corstorphine Dovecot is not as old as Corstorphine Castle but undoubtedly was closely associated with it. Whilst the dovecot has survived, nothing remains of the castle. In relation to modern street names it stood on ground now occupied by bungalows in Castle Avenue to the south of the Dovecot Road entrance to St Margaret's Park. When the castle was built in the fourteenth century it occupied a most important position in the western defences of Edinburgh, protected on the east by Corstorphine Loch and on the west by Gogar Loch. In its heyday it was a most impressive fortress, surrounded by a moat, with an interior courtyard protected by solid curtain walls and massive towers on each corner. In recent years one or two small artefacts have been unearthed by people with garden ground near where the castle stood. By far the most important relic, however, is the lintel, bearing the carved armorial shields of the Forrester and Preston families. It contains three raised shields commemorating the marriage of Henry Forrester and Helenor Preston of Craigmillar. The centre shield bears the initials HP and the three unicorns of the Preston family, while the outer shields bear the initials HF and the three hunting horns of the Forrester family. Around 1750 the lintel was built into a fireplace at Amulree House (later known as The Mansion House) at the north-west end of Corstorphine High Street and remained there until the house was demolished in the 1950s, when the lintel was removed to The Cedars on the north-west corner of St John's Road and Manse Road. When The Cedars was demolished in 1994 the lintel stone was removed to No. 5 Gordon Road.

Towards the west end of Dovecot Road is the south entrance to St Margaret's Park which forms an integral part of the old village walk. It is a public park with the usual municipal attractions of a bowling green and tennis courts. Most of the historical interest, however, is located along its northern boundary where it abuts the High Street. In the north-east corner of the park is the fifteenth or sixteenth-century Dower House which is thought to have been one of the prebendal manses, probably used by one of the canons of the collegiate church, though altered on several occasions since its original construction. It is

The Dower House *c.* 1980, in the north-east corner of St Margaret's Park, dates
from the late fifteenth or early sixteenth century. It is now used as the headquarters of the Corstorphine Trust.
Courtesy of the Corstorphine Trust.

now a three-storey building with crowstepped gables and entrance on the north wall. The exterior is harled with the corner stones exposed, the skewputs still jutting out at a lower level, indicating that the wall-head has been raised at some time in the past to form another storey. Internally much of the house has been modernised but there are two fine wood-panelled rooms, one with a moulded fireplace. At one time the house was known as Gibson Lodge after Dame Henrietta Watson, Lady Gibsone of Pentland, who owned it. The name of the house is usually spelt differently to the family name. The Dower House was extensively damaged by fire in 1991 but has subsequently been restored, and is now used as the headquarters of the Corstorphine Trust.

The Thomson family at the Dower House (Gibson Lodge) in the 1890s. Seated are Robert Currie Thomson (born at Gibson Lodge in 1824 and died there in 1903) and his wife Margaret Thomson, née Manners, born 1828. Standing, from left to right, are Margaret, Catherine, Alexander, Helen and Hugh. R. C. Thomson's parents moved to Corstorphine from Edinburgh about 1821 and were tenants at Gibson Lodge by 1824. The family were market gardeners in Corstorphine for three generations until the 1920s.
Courtesy of Andrew B. Eadie and the Corstorphine Trust.

We now leave St Margaret's Park by the main or north entrance which is marked by imposing gate pillars erected when the ground was gifted to the Parish Council in 1915 by the Honourable Christopher Douglas Brown of Arizona, whose wife Margaret Dixon came from a long-established Corstorphine family.

ST MARGARET'S PARK	ST MARGARET'S PARK
PRESENTED BY	OPENED BY
C. DOUGLAS BROWN	MARGARET DOUGLAS BROWN
JULY 1915	JULY 1915
(EASTMOST PILLAR)	(WESTMOST PILLAR)

It is Christopher Douglas Brown's initials 'CDB' which we saw on the Oakland plaque of 1904 built into the Old Black Bull Inn at the east end of the village. Near the park gates there are a few other buildings within sight which have contributed to Corstorphine's ancient history.

One well-dressed youngster sits it out at the official opening of St Margaret's Park, July 1915.
Courtesy of the Corstorphine Trust.

Just inside the park railings is the local Scout Hut, built on the remnants of Cross Cottages which stood on the site until they were demolished for road widening in 1929. The cottages took their name from the Cross of Corstorphine, a group of five old elm trees arranged in a square with one in the centre, which stood between the cottages and the school. The original Cross has long since disappeared along with the market which was held there for the sale of cattle, pigs and horses, but the trees are clearly depicted in the old colours of the Corstorphine Friendly Society, constituted in August 1789. A new Cross of Corstorphine, consisting of five rowan trees, was planted in 1987 by the children of Corstorphine Primary School. It is located on the grass in the north-west corner of the park. A few hundred yards west of the park gates is one of the oldest domestic houses in Corstorphine village, Claycot, a two-storey white dwelling now incorporated in a modern housing development. At the extreme west end of the village several large flat stones in the wooded area to the south-east of Dunsmuir Court are all that remain of the ancient Physic Well, famed for its medicinal qualities. The stones were moved north-westwards from their previous position on the Stank when it was piped in 1972. In its heyday in the mid-eighteenth century, such was the attraction of the well for the people of Edinburgh that a coach ran specially between the city and Corstorphine, making eight or nine journeys each weekday and four journeys on a Sunday. In 1750 trade was so good that a Leith wood merchant decided to build Amulree House to accommodate overnight guests. Unfortunately, when the Stank ditch nearby was deepened to improve drainage, there was an interruption of the water supply to the well, with the result that his investment, like the water, showed little or no return.

Corstorphine Primary School is on the north side of the High Street, immediately opposite St Margaret's Park. The earliest record of a school in the village is 1646. It was established by George the first Lord Forrester in rather humble surroundings near Albyn Cottage at the east end of the village. In 1819 a new school was built on the present site, described then as 'ground occupied by cottars on the north side of the Cross of Corstorphine'. A major extension was built in 1848 and rebuilt in 1894, more than twenty years after the first meeting of the School Board of Corstorphine on 26th April 1873. All these developments have taken place at the present location. Looked at from the

High Street, the original 1819 school is the lower storey of the right-hand section. A date plaque, 1848, appears on the east gable and a further plaque, REBUILT 1894, can be seen on the south-facing frontage.

On 12th September 1996 there was a celebration of the 350th anniversary of the founding of the school which has a record of the headmasters and headteachers back to 1646. The event was marked by the children releasing hundreds of helium-filled balloons which were purchased at £1 each to raise funds to instal benches in the playground. The main celebration, however, took place in May 1996 to coincide with the 10th Corstorphine Fair. A pageant was held in the playground where six flat-loading lorries were provided, on which the children performed historical sketches. The school orchestra played a selection of music from various periods over the school's history, and the children were dressed in costumes appropriate to the period.

The last section of the old village walk lies between Manse Road and Corstorphine Kirk. On the north side of the High Street a small lane gives access to a feu of ground acquired by Corstorphine United Free Church in 1930. At the Union of the United Free Church and the Church of Scotland in 1929 those of the Free congregation who were opposed to the Union formed a congregation of their own and worshipped in the Masonic Hall for the first few months. When the new church hall was opened for worship on 5th June 1930, there was a membership of 51, but by 1935 the congregation was sufficiently established to call its first minister of full status, Rev. Robert Waugh. In the years that followed, the congregation increased substantially and set up a Sunday School, Choir, Prayer Union and Temperance Association.

To the east of the lane leading to the United Free Church is a three-storey tenement block with the date 1910 over the entrance. This marks the approximate location of the Tron Tree at which a market was at one time held for the sale of farm produce, including the celebrated delicacy Corstorphine Cream. The *Old Statistical Account of Scotland* records the mystery of its preparation:

> They put the milk, when fresh drawn, into a barrel or wooden vessel, which is submitted to a degree of heat, generally by immersion in warm water, this accelerates the stage of fermentation. The serous is separated from the other parts of the milk, the oleaginous and coagulable; the serum is drawn off by a hole in the lower part

→ what happen after with them?

The pupils of Corstorphine Primary School released hundreds of helium-filled balloons in the playground on 12th September 1996 to mark 350 years of education in the old village.
Photograph by Jenni Wood.

of the vessel; what remains is put into the plunge-churn and after being agitated for some time, is sent to market as Corstorphine Cream.

At one of the Corstorphine Fairs in recent years, Corstorphine Cream was recreated specially for the event, but it has not gone into commercial production.

Although it is many years since Corstorphine Cream was sold at the Tron Tree, other processes of fermentation have lost little to history: the Corstorphine Inn, with its famous skittle alley, is the only remaining hostelry in the old village. The last building in the High Street takes us back to the beginning of the walk. Corstorphine Parish Church Hall,

Corporation motor bus at the junction of St John's Road and Station Road, Corstorphine in 1922.
Courtesy of D. L. G. Hunter.

adjacent to the churchyard, occupies the site of the house built in 1550 and used by the provost of the collegiate church. When the old house was demolished in the 1880s, the inscribed skewstones were preserved and built into the gable of the church hall.

Corstorphine's 'high' village, as it became known, grew up along the line of St John's Road from the mid-nineteenth century. Today it is the commercial centre of the immediate district with numerous shops, offices, pubs and restaurants. The most prominent landmark is the Gothic spire of St Ninian's Parish Church, erected as a Free Church in 1870 on the site of an earlier Free Church dating from 1844. Adjacent to it, but entered from St Ninian's Road, is the Roman Catholic Church of St John the Baptist, its clean modern lines creating an interesting contrast with the Gothic Revival architecture of St Ninian's. St John's was designed by Charles W. Gray and was opened for worship in 1963 by Cardinal Gordon Gray. Corstorphine's rich heritage of churches also includes St Anne's Parish Church on the north-west corner of St John's Road and Kaimes Road. The rather plain exterior of rough-faced Hailes stone in regular courses, and the absence of the campanile or tower above the entrance doorway, belies an interior of much greater detail by the architect, P. Macgregor Chalmers.

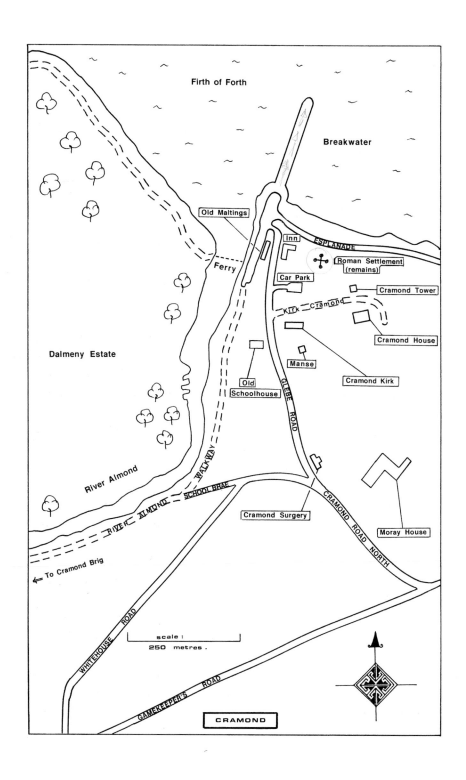

Firth of Forth

Breakwater

Old Maltings

Inn ESPLANADE

Ferry

Roman Settlement
(remains)

Car Park

Cramond Tower

Kirk Cramond

Cramond House

Dalmeny Estate

Old
Schoolhouse

Manse

Cramond Kirk

GLEBE ROAD

WALKWAY

River Almond

SCHOOL BRAE

RIVER ALMOND

Cramond Surgery

CRAMOND ROAD NORTH

Moray House

To Cramond Brig

WHITEHOUSE ROAD

scale :
250 metres.

GAMEKEEPER'S ROAD

CRAMOND

CHAPTER TWO

Cramond

Cramond village lies four miles north-west of Princes Street at the mouth of the River Almond where it flows into the Firth of Forth. Its picture-postcard image is in contrast to its ancient history. In the second century A.D. it was a Roman defence post; in the eighteenth century it created its own industrial revolution in the Almond valley; and in the early nineteenth century much of the oldest part of the village was demolished to enable Lady Torphichen to extend the policies of Cramond House. Nor has it yet revealed its full potential. In 1995 excavations to the north of Cramond Kirk unearthed the earliest known settlement site in Lothian to date, stretching back more than 6000 years to the Mesolithic or Middle Stone Age period. Also in 1995, a cist, dating from around 1500 B.C., was found during building work at Marwood, Whitehouse Road. It was recovered almost intact and now forms part of a permanent exhibition at Cramond Heritage Trust, The Maltings, Cramond Harbour. The greatest find to date, however, was in January 1997 when the local ferryman, Robert Graham, spotted a statue of a lioness sticking out of the mudbanks of the River Almond. The statue has been identified as a Roman funeral relic which probably decorated a mausoleum more than 1500 years ago.

The village, with its old Kirk dating back many centuries, was at one time the biggest centre of population in the parish of Cramond, which stretched from Granton to Turnhouse. The decline and eventual fall of the mills in the mid-nineteenth century, and the departure of the minister, kirk session and many of the congregation to the new Cramond Free Church at Davidson's Mains following the Disruption in 1843, all contributed to a gradual decline in the relative importance of Cramond. The Kirk continued after the Disruption, but it no longer had an ecclesiastical monopoly, and matters such as the relief of the poor and education passed into secular hands. This gradual decline became progressively more obvious in the road transport era of the early twentieth century on account of Cramond's geographical position.

Today Cramond lies peacefully at the northern edge of its attractive suburban hinterland, conscious of its unique heritage, and able to bring

This aerial view of Cramond, taken in 1976, shows the ferryman's cottage in the lower right-hand corner. Towards the top of the picture is Cramond Kirk and Kirkyard, to the far left of which is Cramond House. Excavations of Roman remains can be seen near the car park on the left.
Courtesy of The Scotsman Publications Ltd.

more of it to the attention of its many visitors. There are two main walks: the first is a tour of the old village; the second is more extensive: to locate what remains of the mill industries along the banks of the River Almond between Cramond Inn and Cramond Brig Hotel. Additional information for visitors is available from Cramond Heritage Trust, The Maltings, Cramond Harbour.

The name Cramond is derived from *caer Amond*, a fortified place on the Almond.

THE VILLAGE WALK

Cramond is usually approached from Cramond Road North past the former Dunfermline College of Physical Education (now Moray House Institute of Education, Heriot Watt University) designed by Robert Matthew, Johnson-Marshall & Partners in 1964. A few hundred yards north, Cramond Glebe Road leads down to the old village from the new Health Centre, built on the site of Laidlaw's tearoom and market garden. On the left-hand side the substantial white harled house, with its gable end facing the street, announces on the timber gates its historical past – The Old Schoolhouse. It was built for £148:16:6 in 1778 to replace an earlier ruinous building nearer to the Kirk. The ground floor contained a large schoolroom and a private room for the schoolmaster, and on the upper floor there were four additional rooms. Its first master was Ninian Paton who had taught at the old school since 1764. Opposite the old schoolhouse is Cramond Manse, built in extensive policies to the south of Cramond Kirk in 1745.

Cramond Kirk is considerably older than the manse: in fact there has been some form of ecclesiastical building on the site almost from time immemorial. It is probable that the old Roman fort was used by Christian communities in the sixth century before a more permanent building was erected. Very little is known about the early Christian community except that it came within the jurisdiction of the Bishop of Dunkeld, ecclesiastical superior of the parish, and feudal superior of Nether Cramond. It is known that there had been a medieval church on the site, but it had become ruinous by 1656. A new church was built in that year incorporating the fifteenth-century tower at the west end, and the Cramond vault at the east end, later set aside as the burial place of the Inglis of Cramond. Several additions and alterations have

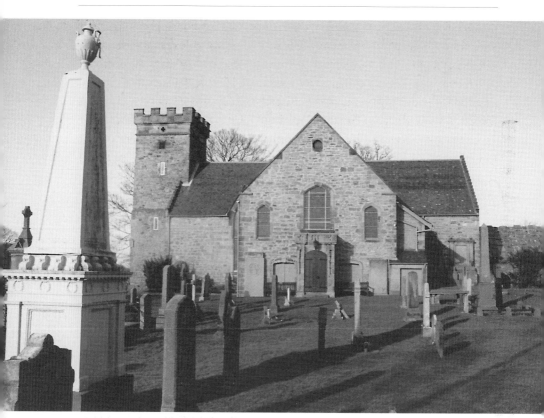

Cramond Kirk was rebuilt in 1656 on the site of a medieval church which had become ruinous. The new church incorporated the fifteenth-century west tower, and the Cramond vault at the east end.
Photograph by Jenni Wood.

been made to the church since 1656. In 1701 the north aisle was enlarged to the west, and the south aisle was enlarged to the south, to form the Barnton vault, which contains the body of John, Earl of Selkirk and Ruglen, one-time Master of the Mint in Scotland, who died in 1744. A little more than a century after the 1701 additions, the stone-masons were busy again, in 1811, under the direction of the architect Robert Burn. Further nineteenth-century alterations were done by William Burn in 1828, Robert Bell in 1843 and David Bryce in 1851 and 1868. The distinctive castellated parapet was added round the fifteenth-century church tower, and more space was created in the interior. Less significant alterations were made during the remainder of the nineteenth century but it was not until 1911 that the church began to take on its present-day appearance. The north aisle was completely rebuilt and an organ chamber was constructed east of the south aisle. Internally almost all the fabric dates from 1911. Various contributions to *Cramond*, a book published by Cramond Heritage Trust, provide an interesting insight into the social history of the parish as seen through the minutes of the Kirk Session meetings, which date back to 1651. The sabbath was observed by most people, with a substantial part of the day taken up by the main church service which lasted anything up to three or four hours. The local gentry and their families sat in comparative comfort in the small galleries, whilst the ordinary folk sat either on the floor or on whatever small stool they brought with them. The prospect of more than three hours' continuous worship tended to create an atmosphere of general informality, although there were limits which had to be enforced, as the occasion arose:

> The Session considering that divine service is disturbed by ye fighting of doges in ye Church on the Sabbath dayes therefore they appoint ye Beddell to beat yaim out of ye Church, and also to speake to the people that they keep them at home behind yaim on the Sabbath dayes (3rd December 1691).

The sermon began with an hour-long reading from the scriptures by the precentor, who was usually also the local schoolmaster and session clerk. When he had completed his chosen text, the minister continued the service with two hours of preaching, broken by occasional prayers. A significant part of the proceedings dealt with penitents who were required to sit on the cutty stool, set on a raised platform, to be publicly rebuked for their misdemeanours. The offences covered the full range of human activity: adultery, drunkenness, breach of the peace and failure to attend church, but, strangely, no recorded cases of witchcraft.

Cramond Churchyard has a variety of stones of different ages and styles. Many show the symbols of death – skulls, bones, hourglasses and the Green Man, whilst others carry the symbols of immortality – the winged soul and the angel. There are several examples of the Green Man, depicted as human or cat-like faces, frequently with ugly teeth, protruding tongues, and greenery sprouting from the cheeks, forehead, nose or mouth. The oldest legible stone is to John Stalker, on the east wall, who died on 6th February 1608. Only the briefest selection of

In a quiet corner of Cramond Kirkyard rich detail is arranged around the twin
Corinthian columns of the Howison Crauford tombstone.
Photograph by Graham C. Cant.

other interesting stones can be included here: on the south wall of the church a large plain slab dated 1687 for George Sheiell, Fearmour in Grotthill; on the north boundary wall a polished granite stone with perpendicular 'church window' tracery for the Rev. Walter Laidlaw Colvin D.D., minister at Cramond immediately after the Disruption in 1843, until his death in 1877; and on the south wall two interesting monuments, appropriately made of iron, commemorating members of the Cadell family who owned the iron mills in the Almond valley during the eighteenth and nineteenth centuries. One is to William Cadell who died in 1844 at the age of twenty-four, and the other recalls the passing, in 1851, of Anne Wilson who, as a young woman, married one of the iron masters.

To the north of Cramond Kirk, on Cramond Glebe Road, is the entrance to Kirk Cramond, marked by old pillars and a small, lintelled iron gateway no longer in use. Kirk Cramond leads to open parkland where the remains of a Roman fort were excavated between 1954 and 1966. The grassed area of Kirk Cramond is open to the public, but Cramond Tower is private property and Cramond House belongs to the General Trustees of the Church of Scotland. Both the tower and the house have a long and interesting history.

Cramond Tower is a tall medieval defensive structure of uncertain date, commanding magnificent views of Cramond Island and the Firth of Forth. One theory is that it was part of the Palace of the Bishop of Dunkeld who held the lands of Cramond from King David I in the twelfth century. Documentary evidence supports the contention that Robert de Cardney, Bishop of Dunkeld, exchanged his lands of Cammo in 1409 for Cramond Tower, then owned by John de Nudre. In 1574 James Paton sold the tower to Archibald Douglas of Kilspindie, who later sold it to Alexander Douglas. It was Alexander Douglas who eventually sold the property to the first of the Inglis family in 1622. Whether the tower was ever the Bishop's Palace, as suggested by John Philp Wood, is a matter of conjecture. There is certainly evidence of some building structure adjacent to it, both on the east side and on the west side. According to Wood's account in 1794, the building to the east was the Bishop's Palace, and that to the west was the Chapel. An archaeological excavation carried out to the west of the tower in 1977 failed to prove Wood's contention. It did, however, show the existence of another building, although not directly abutting the tower itself. Later

Cramond Tower, a tall medieval defensive structure of uncertain date, quietly reflects upon its great antiquity.
Photograph by Jenni Wood.

excavations on the east side revealed mortared wall foundations suggesting a rectangular addition to the tower. Although the mystery remains unsolved, perhaps the most tantalising evidence is the easily observed raggled stonework high up on the east and west walls. During the excavations several finds were made which, although interesting in themselves, did not assist in proving the existence of any other building. Among the finds were the remains of a seventeenth-century wine bottle marked 'Cramond' and a coin of the reign of Charles II (1660–1685).

Cramond Tower seems to have flourished under a long line of influential owners up to *c.*1680 when the Inglis family moved out to Cramond House nearby, but it fared less well in the years that followed. A watercolour by James Skene in 1837 shows the tower in ruins, and MacGibbon and Ross, in *The Castellated and Domestic Architecture of Scotland* (1889), say: 'it [the Tower] is in an unfortunate condition being entirely crowned with ivy which has got such a hold of it (the branches in some places going through the walls) as to greatly imperil its safety'. The tower lay in that state until the 1960s, when Edinburgh Corporation began restoration work which they quickly abandoned shortly thereafter on discovering that they were not actually the owners. In 1978 Cramond Tower was acquired by George Jamieson, the wildlife artist and taxidermist, who set about a comprehensive programme of restoration with advice from Robert Hurd and Partners and the Historic Buildings Council. The result is a most interesting four-storey building of rough stone finish with a projecting stairtower on the south-east corner, all capped with a slated roof but without the encumbrances of rhones and downpipes. Internally each of the four floors has been extensively renovated. The ground floor, previously below ground level and reached by a short flight of stone steps, has been given a wooden floor and is used by Mr Jamieson as a gallery. On the floor above, the main hall has a restored arched fireplace with a canopy and chimney breast, and Georgian windows have been fitted in each wall except the north. The main features of the second floor are the window embrasure with stone seats, and the garderobe built into the thickness of the east wall: the top floor provides bedroom and bathroom accommodation. In 1992 a modern wing was built to the east in a style sympathetic to the main tower.

Cramond House, lying between Cramond Churchyard and Cramond Tower, dates from about 1680. The history of its development is most

The east front of Cramond House, built in the 1770s, is reached by a spreading flight of steps with square balusters. From the entrance doorway there is a fine view, down a broad avenue of trees, to Berwick Law in the distance.
Photograph by Jenni Wood.

easily understood by studying its H-plan formation: the central block is substantially the house built by John Inglis of Cramond in 1680 shortly before his death. It is three storeys in height, built of harled rubble, with exposed window dressings. How and when the basic house developed first to T-formation, and then H-formation, is a matter on which there are different opinions. There is, however, no doubt about the ordered appearance of its imposing east facade, built in the 1770s and reached by a spreading flight of steps with square balusters. The entire east wing is of two storeys only, of polished ashlar, the main storey, over the basement, being identified by very tall astragalled windows with semi-circular heads. The central part of the frontage projects slightly and carries a pediment with the Inglis crest carved in

stone. From the raised position of the front entrance there is a magnificent view through a broad avenue of trees, taking as its focal point, in
the distance, the summit of Berwick Law in East Lothian. Internally the
most imposing features are in the east wing. The spacious entrance hall
has very high coved ceilings and leads to the stone staircase, lit by a
cupola. Two corresponding rooms lead off the entrance hall, namely
the drawing room to the south, and the dining room to the north. The
staircase leads to the old house, which has a long passage running east
to west, to communicate with the west wing built around 1820.

When the Inglis baronetcy came to an end in 1817 for want of a male
heir, the estate passed to Lady Torphichen, daughter of Sir John Inglis.
The involvement of the families Craigie and Halkett through marriage
made the Craigie-Halketts the new lairds of Cramond in 1849, until
some time after the First World War when the house was in the hands
of the last of the line, Miss Dorothy Craigie-Halkett. Cramond House
was visited by royalty, notably in the summer of 1860 when the
Duchess of Kent, mother of Queen Victoria, resided there. Queen
Victoria, en route for Balmoral, visited the Duchess at Cramond House
and made a return visit in September of the same year when she attended Cramond Kirk along with the Prince Consort.

After the demise of this branch of the Craigie-Halkett family,
Cramond House was ultimately acquired by the General Trustees of
the Church of Scotland in 1971. It is presently leased to the Scottish
Wildlife Trust who use it as their headquarters, and there is also a flat
for the beadle of Cramond Parish Church. Although access is now by
a driveway from Cramond Glebe Road (the West Lodge), the original
entrance is much farther to the south at the sharp dogleg bend in
Cramond Road North. The pedimented archway supports one chimney
breast to serve each of the two single-roomed lodges on either side of
the main carriageway.

Leaving Kirk Cramond and proceeding north on Cramond Glebe
Road, we pass, on the right-hand side, an area of rough grassland
beside the public car park. A few feet below the surface lie the remains
of Cramond's Roman Bath-house which was first excavated in the mid-
1970s. It is the best-preserved Roman site in Scotland with walls
surviving up to five feet high but unfortunately it has not been left open
in view of its vulnerability to damage.

The Romans came to Cramond about A.D. 142 by order of the

In January 1997 the local ferryman, Robert Graham (seen here on the left), located a statue of a lioness projecting from the mudbanks of the River Almond. The statue has been identified as a Roman funeral relic which probably decorated a mausoleum more than 1500 years ago.
Courtesy of The Scotsman Publications Ltd.

Emperor Antoninus Pius to establish a fort at the eastern end of a frontier line across Scotland from the Forth to the Clyde. Cramond was ideally suited to their requirements. Local stone, cut from the valley of the Almond, was plentiful for building; the surrounding land was fertile and capable of further cultivation; and the mouth of the Almond provided sheltered mooring for their boats. A Roman garrison, of probably almost five hundred men, set about the task of building an extensive fort covering almost six acres of ground. Although the presence of the Romans at Cramond had been known about for many years, it was not until 1954 that the fort was discovered. Several years of patient excavation since then have pieced together a substantial part of its history. The various finds have been deposited with Huntly House Museum in the Canongate in central Edinburgh. The fort was rectangular in shape with its long walls or ramparts running north and south. These were built of clay or turf twenty-seven feet thick with a stone facing, and probably fifteen feet high. Gates, flanked by towers, were set in each of the four sides, allowing constant surveillance in every direction. Internally a road running between the east and west gates divided the rectangle into a small section to the north, and a larger section to the south. Located to the north of the road were the workshops, and a latrine; to the south of the road lay the garrison headquarters in the centre, flanked by granaries and the commander's house. Later excavations revealed evidence of buildings outside the protection of the fort, as well as defensive ditches in what is now the Manse garden. To the east an 'industrial estate' has been unearthed, where open-ended sheds provided working facilities for carpenters, ironworkers, tanners and shoemakers.

Until recently it was thought that the Roman occupation of

Cramond Village in 1996 looking west between the old cottages to the River Almond and the ferryman's cottage on the opposite bank.
Photograph by Jenni Wood.

Progress in 1996 is still fairly slow in the old village street beside the seventeenth-century Cramond Inn.
Photograph by Jenni Wood.

Cramond was rather sporadic but archaeological evidence now suggests that they maintained a constant presence for more than forty years before withdrawing and returning at the beginning of the third century A.D. Sometime between A.D. 208 and 211 the army of the Emperor Septimius Severus is recorded at Cramond repairing the fort and improving the roads and drainage, but there is no evidence that Severus was there in person.

Lower down Cramond Glebe Road, the smart white paintwork of Cramond Inn, with the date 1670 above a window, matches exactly Cramond's remaining whitewashed cottages, overlooking the quayside. The Maltings, leased by the local authority to Cramond Heritage Trust, houses a permanent exhibition, *Cramond's Story* from the Mesolithic (Middle Stone Age) period to the present century. The permanent

Information on local walks and places of interest is available at The Maltings, or, alternatively, there is the option of a quiet seat in the sun.
Photograph by Jenni Wood.

exhibits are supplemented each year by smaller exhibitions of topical interest. The Centre is open at week-ends from June to September and by special arrangement at other times. The Trust, honouring Cramond Association's original aim to provide an Interpretation Centre, works with school groups, provides guided tours of the village, and is building a comprehensive archive of material relating to Cramond.

THE RIVERSIDE WALK

The Riverside Walk, along the east bank of the River Almond, is a distance of approximately one mile from Cramond village to Old Cramond Brig. Along the path there are one or two stepped inclines,

The Cramond ferry doing brisk business on a Sunday afternoon in the Spring of 1975.
Courtesy of The Scotsman Publications Ltd.

The Cramond ferry at a much earlier date with Sandy Matthew at the tiller.
Courtesy of Cramond Heritage Trust.

The River Almond, at Cramond *c.* 1900, was a popular venue for young and old alike, long before the promenade was built.
Courtesy of The Scotsman Publications Ltd.

and the going can be soft in wet weather. The route does, however, still retain important remnants of the mills which, at one time, formed an integral part of the local economy. Around 1700 there were five separate mills operating between the village and Cramond Brig. The basic commodity was grain, but in 1752 the Smith & Wright Work Company of Leith took a lease of one of the mills and began a small iron industry, making spades, hoes, chains and anchors. The business was bought in 1759 by the Carron Company of Falkirk, and then by William Cadell Jnr. in 1770. Cadell was a shrewd industrialist who expanded the business, but the valley of the Almond was never an ideal location to

Competitors set sail for the European Hornet Championships at Cramond in
1977. The event was hosted by the Cramond Boat Club.
Courtesy of The Scotsman Publications Ltd.

remain competitive. Access to many of the mills was awkward and the
already meagre water supply was subject to serious interruption during
the summer months. By 1800 the iron industry was in serious
decline and, despite various attempts at diversification (e.g. into
paper), the Cadells' demise came in 1860 through their inability to
remain competitive. After the Cadells the mills were put to a variety of
uses for individual businesses.

Walking upstream from the village, our first port of call, at the foot
of School Brae, is Cockle Mill, now beautifully restored as private
housing. Its name is taken originally from the cockle weed which grows

with corn crops. At the water's edge it is still possible to make out the dock, cut into the river bank, where boats berthed to deposit coal, and to take away the completed products. The next mill upstream is Fairafar, its arched masonry now completely ruinous, lying at the water's edge, beside a well-preserved weir about ten feet high. The square shell is all that remains of the west forge which contained two furnaces and a great tilt hammer. Beyond Fairafar the Almond runs deep and wide past a protruding cliff face which has been conveniently skirted by steps carrying the path high above the river bank. At the highest point there is a seat gifted by the Cramond Association to mark the opening of that part of the walk on 14th May 1966. Farther on, the last two mills lay close to one another: first Peggie's Mill, of which nothing remains; and then Dowie's Mill with the remains of its

A Territorial Army picnic at Cramond, believed to be *c.*1913. At the top right-hand corner of the picture is the horse and carriage which was driven by Hendry Baillie between Cramond and the railway stations at Davidson's Mains and Barnton.
Courtesy of Mrs A. Borthwick.

A Victorian boating scene on the River Almond below Cramond Brig.
Courtesy of Cramond Heritage Trust.

weir. At Dowie's Mill there is an interesting old house with a round-nosed gable, and a row of cottages which it is said date from *c.*1690. Didcock Bros. from Gorgie, the furniture makers, operated from Dowie's Mill from 1916 to 1936. A short walk upstream from the mill is Old Cramond Brig (now restricted to pedestrians only) which once carried the main road from Edinburgh to South Queensferry. Believed to date from 1500, the bridge carries dates, 1687, 1761, 1776 and 1854, being the years in which it was 'repaired by both shires', i.e. Linlithgowshire and Edinburghshire. The date 1619, on the outer side of the west parapet, is better viewed from the safety of the embankment. The Brig's greatest claim to fame is, of course, its legendary connection with Jock Howison. According to Sir Walter Scott, King James V was strolling, incognito, across Old Cramond Brig when he was suddenly

Carriages await the arrival of the next train at Barnton Station, formerly at the
south end of Whitehouse Road. To the left of the station is the clubhouse of the
Royal Burgess Golfing Society.

set upon by a marauding gang. Without knowing the identity of the
King, young Jock came to the rescue and took King James into his
cottage where he dressed his wounds and sent him on his way. When
the King returned to Holyrood he sent for Howison, revealed his identity, and rewarded Jock with a grant of land in gratitude for his
courage. The lands of Braehead were actually granted to the Howisons
in 1465 during the reign of James III (1460–1488).

At this point in the walk we are within a stone's throw of Cramond
Brig Hotel – a convenient place to stop. An alternative route is by Brae
Park Road, past the small plaque on the right which commemorates Pet
Marjorie (1802–1811). Marjory Fleming was born on 15th January
1803, the third child of James Fleming, an accountant in Kirkcaldy, and
his wife Isabella. Marjory died before reaching her ninth birthday but
left a fascinating collection of works, including three journals, some
verses and a few letters, all written in the last three years of her life. *Pet
Marjorie* was included with *Rab and his Friends* and other short sto-

ries in a volume of essays and sketches under the title *Leisure Hours* by Dr John Brown, physician and author.

At the top of Brae Park Road, opposite its junction with Whitehouse Road, twin-arched gate piers, with curtain walls pierced by arrow slits, once led to Barnton House. A left turn into Whitehouse Road takes us back to Cramond Glebe Road.

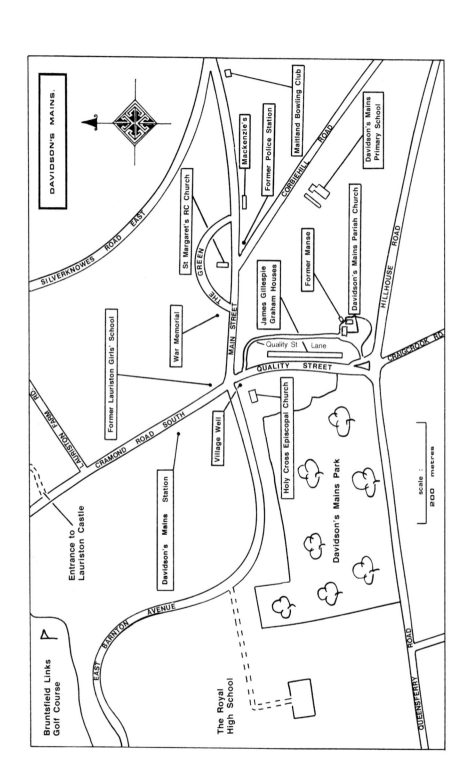

DAVIDSON'S MAINS.

Bruntsfield Links
Golf Course

Entrance to
Lauriston Castle

LAURISTON FARM RD

SILVERKNOWES ROAD EAST

CRAMOND ROAD SOUTH

EAST BARNTON AVENUE

The Royal
High School

Davidson's Mains   Station

Former Lauriston Girls' School

War Memorial

St Margaret's RC Church

THE GREEN

MAIN STREET

Village Well

QUALITY STREET

Quality St   Lane

James Gillespie
Graham Houses

Former Manse

Davidson's Mains Parish Church

Holy Cross Episcopal Church

Davidson's Mains Park

CRAIGCROOK RD

Mackenzie's

Former Police Station

Maitland Bowling Club

CORBIEHILL   ROAD

Davidson's Mains
Primary School

HILLHOUSE   ROAD

QUEENSFERRY   ROAD

scale :
200   metres

CHAPTER THREE

Davidson's Mains

Davidson's Mains lies three miles north-west of Princes Street, and about one mile short of the village of Cramond. It is not one of Edinburgh's oldest villages, but it does retain much of its original layout, and some of its earliest houses and cottages. The village, originally known as Muttonhole, undoubtedly owes its origin to the junction of two important highways, namely the roads from Leith and from Edinburgh to Queensferry and to Cramond. Ferry Road, from Leith, entered the village at its east end and joined the road from Edinburgh, which came through Blackhall and entered the village by what is now Corbiehill Road. Subsequent development, particularly after 1843, was in many respects greatly influenced by the relative decline of Cramond as the centre of population and activity in the parish. The other great influence of the late nineteenth century was, of course, the railway which crossed under Ferry Road and ran in a double track, north of Main Street, to Davidson's Mains Station and Barnton Station. With the improvement of road transport in the early twentieth century, Davidson's Mains, in common with many other outlying communities, continued its gradual integration into the City of Edinburgh. At the present day, the main street retains a village or community atmosphere, at the centre of a wide residential neighbourhood.

Davidson's Mains was known as Muttonhole until about 1850. The date of origin of the name is uncertain but it is recorded at least as early as 1669. The derivation of the name Muttonhole is also shrouded in mystery: one theory suggests a hollow in which sheep were slaughtered; but, on the other hand, variations of the name exist in other parts of Scotland, and the ending may be *hall* rather than *hole*. In the latter part of the nineteenth century the name gradually changed to Davidson's Mains, taken from the Davidson family who owned the mansion of Muirhouse in Marine Drive.

Davidson's Mains, from the air, looking south in 1973. Queensferry Road runs from left to right and meets Quality Street at the junction near the top of the picture. To the left of Quality Street is Davidson's Mains Parish Church, and to the right is the Public Park. Part of the grounds of Lauriston Castle can be seen at the bottom of the photograph

Crown Copyright: Royal Commission on the Ancient and Historical Monuments of Scotland.

THE VILLAGE WALK

The village walk is comparatively short, on even ground, and almost devoid of steep inclines. A separate visit to Lauriston Castle nearby is described later in the chapter. Our walk begins on Corbiehill Road along the traditional route from Edinburgh. Both sides of the street are now lined by pre-Second World War villas, but in the days before Queensferry Road was realigned Corbiehill Road was a narrow country road with farmland on each side. Today the first building of importance, on the left-hand side, is Davidson's Mains Primary School, designed by the City Architect's Department and opened on Tuesday 25th April 1967 by the Right Rev. R. Leonard Small, then Moderator of the General Assembly of the Church of Scotland. The 1967 building replaced Davidson's Mains' first Board School, constructed on the

Davidson's Mains Primary School, designed by the City Architect's Department, was opened on Tuesday 25th April 1967 by the Right Rev. R. Leonard Small, then Moderator of the General Assembly of the Church of Scotland. It was built on the same site as the previous school dating from 1874.
Photograph by Jenni Wood.

William Bannerman, headmaster, and his wife Agnes outside the first Davidson's Mains School in Corbiehill Road in 1909.
Courtesy of A.W. Bannerman.

same site in 1874. All that remains of it is a solitary pillar incorporated in the low boundary wall near the entrance gate. Prior to 1874 there were two other village schools: one was the Free Church School and the other was Lauriston School for Girls under the patronage of the Ramsays of Barnton.

A few hundred yards north, Corbiehill Road meets the Main Street of the old village where the police station (now a fish and chip shop) stood on the east corner. The east section of the village contains diverse points of interest: St Margaret's Roman Catholic Church; the Maitland Bowling Club; the former MacKenzie's Bar, now the Village Inn; and, at the extreme end of the village, the old single-arched stone bridge built around 1890 to carry the road over the railway.

In the mid-nineteenth century Davidson's Mains had a significant Irish population, many of whom were members of the Roman Catholic

St Margaret's Roman Catholic Church in Main Street was designed by Sir Peter Whitson, and opened on 26th April 1953.
Photograph by Jenni Wood.

One of the village smiddies was run by John Macdonald, horseshoer and general blacksmith, at the east end of the village.
Courtesy of Mrs Sadie Fraser.

Church. The parish of St Margaret's was established in 1882, the first priest being Father Michael James Turner who served Davidson's Mains and South Queensferry until 1889. Meetings were held first at Cramond, later at No. 5 Quality Street, and then in a new chapel built on the north side of Main Street about fifty yards west of the present westmost entrance to The Green. In 1952 St Margaret's made a move to their present building, farther east on Main Street, almost opposite the junction with Corbiehill Road. This tall triangle of modern church architecture (considered to be well before its time in 1952) was designed by Sir Peter Whitson, in a style substantially repeated in his later design for St Mark's Roman Catholic Church in Oxgangs Avenue. The foundation stone was laid on 27th April 1952 by Archbishop Gordon J. Gray (later Cardinal Gray), and the church was opened on 26th April 1953. A stone plaque taken from the old chapel farther down Main Street was inserted in the wall commemorating an early benefactor:

Erected by the Catholics of Davidson's Mains in Loving Memory of Matilda Justina Davidson of Tulloch wife of Colonel Craigie

Halkett of Cramond and Harthill the Founder and Pious
Benefactor of this Mission on whose Soul Sweet Jesus have Mercy.

At the east end of the village the Maitland Bowling Club lies to the
south of the road as it crosses the railway line. The club was formed in
1899, taking its name from the Maitland family, superiors of the
ground, who leased it to the club for five shillings per annum. The club
emblem is a ram's head linking the club with the old name of
Muttonhole. A new clubhouse was built in 1923, and the green was
extended in 1928. Past proprietors of the adjacent Muirhouse Arms
(later MacKenzie's and now the Village Inn), particularly Messrs.
Twiss, McLaren and MacKenzie, have taken a keen interest in, and
been elected President of the Maitland Bowling Club. The Muirhouse
Arms was renamed MacKenzie's in tribute to James MacKenzie, born
in 1901 in Tollcross, who became a barman at the pub in 1925, bought
the business in 1932, and worked there until his retirement in 1965.

The west section of Main Street, from Corbiehill Road to Quality
Street, retains some semblance of 'village' housing on its south side, but
much less so on the north side. Over the years the north side has
attracted redevelopment in the form of The Old Inn, the Clydesdale
Bank and new housing in The Green. The west approach to The Green
is the approximate location of the Hawkeree, an old building demolished many years ago, which is believed to have taken its name from
the place where the falconers kept their birds in the days when
Cramond Regis was a hunting estate. In 1995 a War Memorial, in the
form of a single, stone obelisk on a short plinth, was erected in honour
of those who died in two World Wars.

At the west end of Main Street, the mini roundabout at the junction
with Quality Street and Cramond Road South marks an early focal
point in the development of Davidson's Mains. Prior to 1823 the main
road to Cramond Brig and South Queensferry came through the village
and proceeded westward through what is now the entrance to
Davidson's Mains Public Park. This route was closed off when a new
section of Queensferry Road was built between the Blackhall junction
and the Barnton Roundabout. The village was bypassed, providing a
rare opportunity to construct a grand new entrance along the line of
Quality Street. This challenge was convincingly met in 1827 by the
architect James Gillespie Graham, who proposed a long line of sym-
metrical elevations for the east side of Quality Street. The plan

Turkeys galore being herded into The Green in 1934, to be sold later in
Whiteford's shop which can be seen in the background. The herders are, from left
to right: David Whiteford, master butcher; Jackie Baillie, shop manager; Miss
Jean McEwen; Davida and Isabel Whiteford; James Keddie; Jimmy Meechan,
fishmonger; and Jim Riddel, street orderly.
Courtesy of Mrs M. M. Morton.

The preceding scene, in 1996, has changed greatly, although the buildings are still
recognisable. The War Memorial on the right was erected in 1995.
Photograph by Jenni Wood.

envisaged a two-storey, slightly projecting, central block, flanked by single-storey terraces with elaborate porches over the front doors, and culminating at each end with two-storey blocks to match the central feature. The project was never implemented, but a few substantial houses with basement flats, designed by Gillespie Graham, were built at the south end of Quality Street. About the time that Quality Street was built, it was the practice of villagers to cut across the Barnton House policies to collect water from one of the springs on Corstorphine Hill. The habit was objected to by the estate owners, as a result of which reservoirs were built along the line of Queensferry Road with supply pipes extending into the village. The old village well, bearing the date 1832, can still be seen at the entrance to the Park.

Davidson's Mains Parish Church lies in the hollow at the south end of Quality Street, but, for the purpose of our walk it is better to

The old village well (to the right of the pedestrians) bears the date 1832. It can be seen at the west end of Main Street beside the entrance to the public park. *Photograph by Jenni Wood.*

Davidson's Mains Parish Church, at the south end of Quality Street Lane, was established in 1843 as a Free Church by dissenters from Cramond Parish Church. *Photograph by Jenni Wood.*

approach it by Quality Street Lane. The church has its roots in the historic Disruption of 1843, when dissenters, like Dr Muirhead and the entire Kirk Session, left Cramond Kirk to set up Cramond Free Church in Davidson's Mains. The first congregational meeting was held on 21st May 1843. Shortly thereafter, a piece of ground was secured for David Cousin's small church in the Gothic style. The adjacent parish school was built in 1846, and in 1866 the church bellcote was added to complete Cousin's original plan. Cramond Free became Cramond United Free in 1900, Davidson's Mains United Free in 1927 and Davidson's Mains at the time of the Union with the Church of Scotland in 1929. The church has served the community well under a comparatively small number of ministers since 1843. One of the best known was the Rev. David Gibb Mitchell who came to Davidson's Mains in 1890

at the age of thirty-seven, having spent the early part of his life in the
employment of the Caledonian Railway Company. A keen golfer,
cricketer and poet, he is perhaps best remembered as the minister who
delivered many sermons, prayers and readings in 'Braid Scots'. The
church has always had the great advantage of sufficient space around
it to expand its hall accommodation. The large detached hall with the
steeply pitched roof, near the car park, was built in 1964. As you face
the church, the hall, which adjoins the old schoolhouse on the right,
was first constructed in 1933 and extended and renovated in 1995. To
the east of the church, the large, square, two-storey building is the former manse, dating from 1853.

Leaving the church grounds by the short incline near the traffic
lights, we turn right and proceed northwards on Quality Street past the
Gillespie Graham houses. On the west side of the road another church
building sits in its own feu on the corner of Davidson's Mains Public
Park. This is the Scottish Episcopal Church of the Holy Cross in simple Romanesque architecture. Designed in 1912 by J. M. Dick Peddie,
with natural, dressed stone and large brown slates, it contains some
interesting stained glass in the east chancel by Christopher Webb and
two modern stained-glass windows in the nave by Patrick Ross-Smith.
Like so many other churches, its early history was characterised by the
enthusiasm of a handful of people determined to build a strong congregation. A short series of articles on the history of the church has
been written by the Rev. Mary F. Harrison, Deacon at Holy Cross
(great-granddaughter of Sir George Harrison, Lord Provost of
Edinburgh, 1882–1885), in which she traces all the milestones and
relates many of the anecdotes. The first priest, Alfred Griffiths, was
born at Norwood, Surrey on 20th March 1853 and was educated at St
John's College, Cambridge. He was appointed Junior Chaplain at St
Mary's Episcopal Cathedral in Edinburgh in 1887. In addition to his
duties at St Mary's, Mr Griffiths started a fortnightly evensong in 1896
at Cramond Parish Church Hall, the site of which is now occupied by
the offices of J. Smart & Co. (Contractors) Ltd. in Cramond Road
South. Within two years, the nucleus of a congregation had been
formed, and an Iron Church (the Tin Tabernacle as it was called) was
erected on the north-east corner of the present church ground. In 1901
Holy Cross became an Independent Mission with its own constitution,
and two extensions were built onto the Iron Church to accommodate

Church of the Holy Cross.   *Davidson's Mains.*

The 'Tin Tabernacle' was erected *c.* 1898 by the emerging congregation of the Scottish Episcopal Church of the Holy Cross. It was replaced *c.* 1912 by the present stone church, designed by the architect, Dick Peddie. The old village well can be seen on the extreme right of the photograph.

the growing congregation. It was not long, however, before even the extended Tin Tabernacle was found to be inadequate. In 1908 a decision was taken to build a stone church, to seat three hundred, at a cost of £2,500. Several sites were considered but rejected before the architect Mr Dick Peddie drew up definite plans and colour sketches of the proposed building. When work began in November 1912, it seems to have proceeded more quickly than was anticipated, because in May 1913 it was suddenly realised that no ceremony had been arranged for the laying of the foundation stone. The apparent dilemma was quickly resolved, the general view being 'that in view of the advanced state of the building such a ceremony would be rather pointless'. Unfortunately in 1912 ill health compelled Mr Griffiths to resign. When he recovered later and took up an appointment at Prestonpans, the old Iron Church was removed there 'as it was considered that no more fitting use could be found for the church than as a mission under the charge of Mr Griffiths'.

Behind Holy Cross is Davidson's Mains Public Park, extending to thirty-two acres when it was purchased by Edinburgh Corporation in

1922 for £6,500. It is laid out in the grounds of Barnton House, long since demolished. According to Small's *Castles and Mansions of the Lothians*, the original house was built around 1640 by Sir John Smith of Grotthill, Lord Provost of Edinburgh in 1643. In 1788 Lady Glenorchy sold the joint estate of Barnton and Cramond Regis to William Ramsay, banker in Edinburgh, who demolished the old house near Davidson's Mains and built a much grander house nearer the west boundary of the estate. The new house was dominated by a large circular tower of three storeys at the entrance, with a castellated roofline to match a flanking tower of equal proportions. Iron balconies were a feature at second-floor level, particularly round the entrance tower. The Ramsays spent considerable time and effort improving the estate for their own use, and obtained the benefit of having Queensferry Road realigned to the south of its original position. In the days of William Ramsay's grandson, William Ramsay Ramsay, the estate became famous as a sporting park, the laird holding the position of Master of the Linlithgow and Stirlingshire Hunt. Despite the Ramsays' great wealth they were never far from tragedy. William Ramsay Ramsay died young, and his heir died in a carriage accident in 1865, not long after coming of age. The estate was acquired by Sir Alexander Charles Gibson Maitland of Clifton Hall, in 1865, and later passed to the Steel Maitland family who were responsible for selling part of the land to the Caledonian Railway Company, and to the Royal Burgess Golfing Society and Bruntsfield Links Golfing Society. Although Barnton House was demolished many years ago, the west gate piers and curtain wall still stand at the junction of Barnton Avenue West and Whitehouse Road. At the Davidson's Mains entrance to the estate a small lodge house with a thatched roof stood about the position of the police box. The old road, now known as East Barnton Avenue, leads to the Royal High School which was relocated in the mid-1960s from its former building in Regent Road. The school was established in 1128 and throughout its history has produced a long line of able pupils who have achieved great eminence in almost every walk of life – Scott, Cockburn, Bell, Napier, and in more recent years, Norman MacCaig and Ronnie Corbett.

Before concluding our walk, or going on to visit Lauriston Castle, there are two other brief features to mention. The single-storey modern building of the Royal Bank of Scotland sits on the site of the former

The last train to leave Barnton Station on Saturday 5th May 1951.
Courtesy of D. L. G. Hunter.

An early curling scene at Davidson's Mains in February 1945. The rink was to the east of Cramond Road South beside the old railway line to Davidson's Mains Station. The participants are, from left to right, J. Richard S. Crichton, David Whiteford and Matthew Mather, with J. B. Patrick looking on.
Courtesy of Mrs Crichton.

Lauriston School for Girls which played an active part in local education before the passing of the Education Act of 1872, and the resultant
Board School in Corbiehill Road. Farther north on Cramond Road
South the high retaining brick wall at Barnton Avenue marks the position of the railway bridge which carried the line across the road to
Davidson's Mains Station and on to Barnton Station. A hundred yards
ahead, on the right-hand side, is the entrance to Lauriston Castle, open
to the public and well worth a visit.

LAURISTON CASTLE

Lauriston Castle lies to the east of Cramond Road North in a garden
of about thirty acres with magnificient uninterrupted views over the
Firth of Forth and beyond. The Castle, built by Sir Archibald Napier,
dates from the late sixteenth century: a much earlier structure existed
to the east until it was extensively damaged in the Hertford Invasion of
1544. The present building is an interesting amalgam of sixteenth-century towerhouse and Jacobean-style additions by the architect William
Burn in 1824. Gifted to the nation in 1926 by Margaret Johnstone Reid,
Lauriston offers a unique opportunity to appreciate the interior of one
of Edinburgh's grand houses, still furnished in the formal style of the
Reid family.

As suggested in *Lauriston Castle* by Ann Martha Rowan, the architectural history of the castle can best be appreciated by walking round
it in a clockwise direction, beginning on the south side near the original door of the towerhouse. The tall, five-storey towerhouse is
immediately evident on the left, with twin corbelled turrets, ornamental window pediments, and a plethora of dates and inscriptions. To the
right, the long two-storey extension was added by William Burn, the
architect, between 1824 and 1827, which leads to the domestic offices
and stables of the same period. The projecting front porch was added
some time between 1844 and 1854 by Lord Rutherfurd. The north
façade, by Burn also, consists of a long two-storey elevation, incorporating two crowstepped sections, with broad bay windows linked by a
stone balustrade. Slightly to the east of the bell-tower the original
building consisted of one storey only. However, this was altered in
1872 by Thomas MacKnight Crawfurd who added a second storey to
contain the library. The north wall of the library contains two

Visitors relax in a quiet corner of Lauriston Castle, first constructed in the late sixteenth century, and extended in 1824 by the architect, William Burn. *Photograph by Jenni Wood.*

interesting inscriptions. The stone in the curtain wall is a carved panel of 1672 with the arms and motto of the Crawfurd family who brought it to Lauriston after the demolition of their former house at Cartsburn, near Greenock. The other plaque commemorates the gift of Lauriston Castle and its policies to the nation by Mr & Mrs Reid.

Lauriston Castle gives the impression of being a much bigger house than it is, but in fact the reception hall and the six principal rooms are all contained within the first-floor level. The main entrance leads immediately to a flight of stone steps giving access to the reception hall above. This is the focal point of the house, bringing together the original sixteenth-century towerhouse and the elegant extensions of 1827. The principal room in the towerhouse, now greatly altered and renamed the Oak Room, was used by William Robert Reid as a business room. Burn's principal achievement is, however, his north-facing billiard room (now a sitting room), and the drawing room. In a recess on the south wall of the sitting room an elegant bookcase displays the larger part of Mr Reid's collection of Derbyshire fluorspar, known as Blue John. The dining room, now greatly altered from Burn's own design, has a lowered ceiling and oak-grained plaster panelling. To the east of the dining room a corridor leads to the 1872 additions by Thomas MacKnight Crawfurd, the principal feature being the library. Few of the books now on display belonged to the Reids, however, as the bulk of their library was bequeathed to the National Library of Scotland.

Lauriston, over the centuries, has been in the hands of several families, some of whom were important and influential people whilst others appear to have remained in relative obscurity. The Napier family ceased to have any involvement in Lauriston in 1622, after which it was owned by the families Cant, Rigg and then Dalgleish. From 1683 the castle was owned by the Law family, although there is no direct evidence that any of them lived there during more than a century of ownership. By far the most notable of them was John Law, born in 1671, who went to France and became Comptroller General of the Finances of France. When his banking company crashed in 1720, he left France in disgrace and spent the last years of his life in relative poverty. He died in Venice in 1729. Lauriston remained in the hands of the Law family until 1823, after which it changed hands several times during the nineteenth century. Lauriston's closing chapter, however, belongs unreservedly to the Reid family who acquired it in 1902. William Robert Reid, proprietor of Morison & Co., cabinetmakers in Edinburgh, and his wife Margaret both lived at Lauriston with Mrs Reid's brother, William Davidson Barton, until the death of Mr Reid in 1919. Mrs Reid continued to live at Lauriston until her death in 1926 when the house, contents, and grounds were left by her to the nation 'for the use of the public in all time coming and the intelligent education of the public taste'.

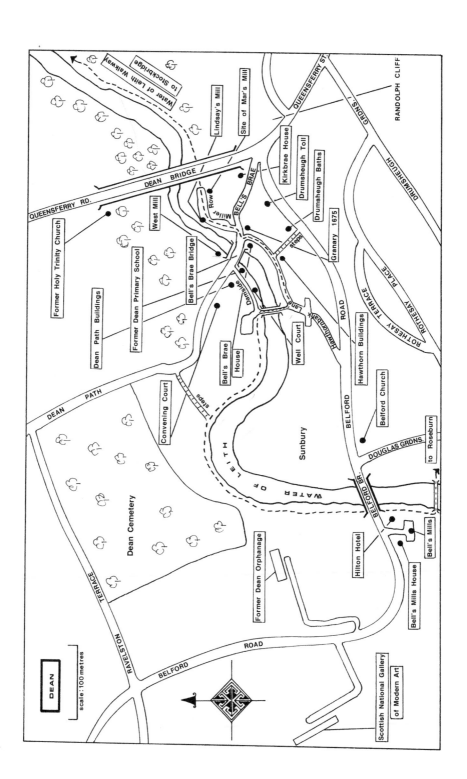

DEAN

scale : 100 metres

RAVELSTON TERRACE

BELFORD ROAD

Dean Cemetery

DEAN PATH

Former Dean Orphanage

Scottish National Gallery of Modern Art

Former Holy Trinity Church

QUEENSFERRY RD.

Dean Path Buildings

Former Dean Primary School

Bell's Brae Bridge

Convening Court

steps

DEAN BRIDGE

West Mill

Miller Row

Bell's Brae House

Drumside

Hamiltonbank Lane

Well Court

WATER OF LEITH

Sunbury

BELFORD ROAD

Hawthorn Buildings

Belford Church

DOUGLAS GRDNS.

to Roseburn

BELFORD BR.

Hilton Hotel

Bell's Mills House

Bell's Mills

Water of Leith Walkway
to Stockbridge

Lindsay's Mill

Site of Mar's Mill

QUEENSFERRY ST.

Kirkbrae House

Drumsheugh Toll

Drumsheugh Baths

Granary 1675

steps

BELL'S BRAE

DRUMSHEUGH GRDNS.

RANDOLPH CLIFF

ROTHESAY PLACE

ROTHESAY TERRACE

CHAPTER FOUR

Dean

From the centre of Edinburgh, Dean is the most accessible of all the villages. It can be reached on foot, within ten minutes of the West End, by way of the west side of Queensferry Street. Most of the places of historic interest are in a fairly compact area. The terrain is steep but fortunately there are some well-positioned public benches.

Dean is one of Edinburgh's most ancient and picturesque villages, lying in comparative repose beneath the tall arches of Telford's Dean Bridge. Modern terminology has caused confusion between two separate communities. The present Dean Village, below the bridge, was once known as Water of Leith Village, whereas Village of Dean was the name given to a separate, much smaller community, on the north side of the river, near the gates to Dean Cemetery. Despite the confusing names it is possible to trace the history of Dean, through its association with the Incorporation of Baxters (i.e. bakers), back to the time of King David I who conferred the profits of the mills on the Abbot and Canons Regular of St Augustine at Holyrood. Early spellings of the name are *den*, *dene* and *denne*, meaning a narrow, winding valley.

At first sight, the visitor to Dean will probably see the centre of the village as a homogeneous group of buildings of uncertain date. In reality, many of the main features have been constructed at widely differing dates, using a variety of materials and architectural styles. With the possible exception of some of the modern additions, the result is, however, visually attractive and greatly enhanced by the natural contours of the ground, which, from time to time, obstruct a full view of a particular building, but compensate with an unexpected glimpse of another.

Dean Village from the air, 1993, looking south. The main buildings of the old village can be seen in the lower half of the picture, with Telford's Dean Bridge on the left leading southwards to the West End of Edinburgh.
Crown Copyright: Royal Commission on the Ancient and Historical Monuments of Scotland.

THE VILLAGE WALK

At the north end of Queensferry Street the main road out of the city centre swings sharply to the right and crosses the Dean Bridge on the way to Blackhall, Barnton and South Queensferry. Two roads strike off to the left, both of which are integral to our walk. Before going down Bell's Brae to the village, however, take a few moments to survey the scene at the higher level. At the far end of the Dean Bridge is the distinctive pinnacled tower of the former Holy Trinity Church, designed by John Henderson in 1838 for the Scottish Episcopal Church. For upwards of a century the building was the home of one of Edinburgh's largest Episcopal congregations, but by 1942 membership had dwindled to a mere handful. At the end of the Second World War the building was used for a while by the German Church, but in the mid-1950s it was sold to an unexpected buyer, the South of Scotland Electricity Board, who used it as a sub-station to serve the West End of Edinburgh. The new owners were held bound to preserve the building but unfortunately the interior was completely stripped in 1957. Around 1989 the Board relinquished control of the building which is again used for religious purposes.

The Dean Bridge was opened to traffic in 1832. By then much of Edinburgh's New Town had been built, but there were large tracts of land lying to the north-west of the city which had not been fully developed owing to the difficulty of access across the deep ravine of the Water of Leith. The old estate of the Nisbets of Dean had been acquired by John Learmonth, Lord Provost of Edinburgh, who decided, in consultation with the Cramond Road Trustees, that a new bridge should be built giving access to his land, which he intended to feu for private building. The Cramond Road Trustees agreed to contribute to the cost on condition that there should be no toll on the bridge and that its design should be approved by Thomas Telford. In the event it was Telford himself who designed it. Work started in October 1829 and, after significant alterations to the plans, to increase the number of arches from three to four, the project was completed in December 1831. When the bridge was opened in the following year, it was described as 'this stupendous structure which forms one of the most splendid monuments in the city'. As far as Telford was concerned, it was certainly a splendid monument which greatly enhanced his reputation, but for

Dean Bridge from the Water of Leith Walkway. The bridge was designed by
Thomas Telford and opened to traffic in 1832.
Photograph by Jenni Wood.

Learmonth it remained a monument for much longer than his financial
predictions had allowed. For upwards of twenty years he waited before
the tide of building work turned again towards further extensions of
the New Town, with the first of the houses being built in Clarendon
Crescent in the 1850s. Today the bridge carries a volume of traffic
which could never have been envisaged by Telford, yet the structure
has remained in excellent condition. This, of course, is due, in no small
way, to frequent maintenance checks both externally and internally.
Access to the inside of the bridge is by a small manhole on the west
pavement. Once inside, it is possible to travel along its length by following its curved arches. Electric light and ventilation holes are fitted
but the sound of the traffic, immediately overhead, can be disconcert-
ing for the uninitiated. From the safety of the pavement there are
spectacular views of the Water of Leith valley below, but the height of
the bridge parapet restricts the use of a camera. Although the bridge

had an excellent accident record during its construction, on completion
it was not long in gaining notoriety as the place

> Where many a man,
> Alas! has ran
>   Here, in an evil hour,
> And cast away
> His life, that day,
>   Beyond all human pow'r.

The poem by Robert McCandless was written *c.* 1888.

As we have already noted, much of Dean Village (or Water of Leith
Village as it was called) was owned or controlled by the Baxters

Kirkbrae House, at the south end of the Dean Bridge, dates from the seventeenth
century and was extended by James Graham Fairley in 1892. At the far side of the
bridge is the former Holy Trinity Church designed in 1838 by John Henderson.
Photograph by Jenni Wood.

(i.e. bakers) of Edinburgh. Several relics of their way of life remain in the village, for example on the walls of Kirkbrae House, an intriguing building which sits at the south end of the bridge at the head of Bell's Brae. The old core of the building, which is believed to date from the seventeenth century, was embellished and extended by James Graham Fairley in 1892 as the residence and office of James Stewart, a prosperous cab hirer. Stewart was a rather quaint, bearded gentleman with a top hat and a ruddy complexion who spent much of the day attending to the business at a pace in keeping with his advancing years. He lived there from 1860 to 1917 when he died at the age of eighty-seven. The building displays several interesting features including a sundial, and pieces of decorated sculpture believed to have come from Dean House. There is also a sculptured panel taken from the ruins of Jericho, a granary built for the Baxters in 1619, which stood in Miller Row immediately below Stewart's house. The upper corners of the panel are occupied by cherubs' heads, between which is a circular garland with the sun in glory at the top and scrolls on each side. Below is the inscription: 'In the sweat of thy face shalt thou eat bread, Gen. 3 verse 19'.

Further down Bell's Brae, but before we cross Bell's Brae Bridge (which once carried the main road out of Edinburgh) there is further evidence of the Baxters' ancient presence. Set into the masonry behind the public bench is a panel bearing two crossed peels (used for extracting hot loaves or cakes from the ovens) and the date 1643. Beside it is a window lintel with the words 'Blesit be God for al his Giftis'. On the opposite pavement, facing down towards the bridge, is a four-storey building with two rectangular stair-turrets. It was built in 1675 as a granary for the Baxters, and later used for the Water of Leith Mission by St Mary's Episcopal Cathedral, before being made into flats by F. R. Stevenson in 1974. Its sculptured panel bears the crossed peels, other heraldic devices, and the legend 'God's Providence is our Inheritans'. On the door lintel are the words 'God bless the Baxters of Edinbrugh who bult this Hous 1675'. Opposite this building is the entrance to Miller Row giving access to the Water of Leith Walkway from Dean to St Bernard's Well and Stockbridge. On the left as we turn down Miller Row are three mill stones (and an information board) set on the remains of Lindsay's Mill. Not much of the building is evident from the higher level, but from the lower level, beside the Water of Leith, substantial masonry walls are still evident. There are door and

Re-enactment of the Feeing of the Baxters outside Bell's Brae House, with the late Mr Basil Skinner, former Director of the Extra-Mural Department of Edinburgh University, presiding.
Courtesy of The Scotsman Publications Ltd.

window spaces and what looks like the sluice archway for the mill water course, now blocked by debris. Opposite the higher level of Lindsay's Mill, the site of Jericho (the origin of the name is unknown) is occupied by a sympathetically designed modern building for a firm of architects and civil engineers. Sheltering beneath the Dean Bridge, the last building, castellated and turreted, was built as a squash court in 1912 on the site of Mar's Mill. In recent years it has had an industrial use.

We now return to Bell's Brae Bridge, where there is one other property on the left, Bell's Brae House, which should not go unnoticed, particularly in view of the effort expended in saving it from demolition.

West Mill, built in 1805 on the banks of the Water of Leith, was restored as flats
by Philip Cocker & Partners in 1973.
Courtesy of Philip Cocker & Partners. Photograph by the late A.L.Hunter.

Originally built in the mid-seventeenth century, its early use is unknown, but in more recent times parts of it were used as a school and as a laundry, before it fell into a serious state of neglect. In 1946 it was bought by the artist Aleksander Zyw, restored by Basil Spence (later Sir Basil Spence), and used by Zyw as his house and studio. Later he had his studio in an old building on the south side of Bell's Brae which had had a smithy on the ground floor and a saddler's shop above. On the far side of Bell's Brae Bridge, with the Water of Leith lapping against its bulky walls, is West Mill, reconstructed from 1805 to 1806 and restored as flats for the Link Housing Association by Philip Cocker & Partners during 1972 and 1973. The names of the Deacons and Masters of the Incorporation of Baxters, at the time of reconstruction, are recorded on a wheatsheaf roundel high up on the south-west wall. The water, which came from a weir upstream of the village, drove two internal wheels, each 18 feet in diameter and 12 feet wide, and was then discharged through two sluice arches, low on the south-east wall, back into the main flow. Immediately downstream, another weir provided water-power for Lindsay's Mill, Mar's Mill and others between here and Canonmills. Also on the north side of the water, opposite West Mill, is the former Dean Primary School opened in 1875 by the Edinburgh School Board. Prior to 1875, most of the village children would probably have attended either one of the small privately-run schools in the vicinity, or Dean Free Church School which was in the basement of the first Dean Free Church, near the east end of Belford Road. Dean Primary School remained the district school until 1961, by which time the roll had decreased substantially. When it closed on 20th January 1961, the remaining thirty-seven pupils were transferred to Flora Stevenson's School at Comely Bank. The school building was converted to flats during 1985 and 1986.

Remaining on the south bank of the Water of Leith, we take the narrow 'high road' known as Hawthornbank Lane. On the left is another of the Dean's unusual styles of architecture, the yellow-ochre half-timbered houses of Hawthorn Buildings, designed by Dunn & Findlay in 1895 and restored by Philip Cocker & Partners in 1978. From the elevated pathway there is a fine view of Well Court on the opposite bank, its turreted oriel windows jutting out towards the water. This development was the idea of John Ritchie Findlay, philanthropic owner of *The Scotsman*, who had it built in 1884 as an experiment in model

Hawthorn Buildings, in Hawthornbank Lane, was designed by Dunn & Findlay in 1895 and restored by Philip Cocker & Partners in 1978.
Photograph by Jenni Wood.

housing for working people. The architect was Sydney Mitchell, who designed it to be seen from Mr Findlay's own house in Rothesay Terrace on the high ground to the south of the village. At the lower end of Hawthornbank Lane the area of ground between the iron footbridge and Belford Road was called the High Green. For many years it remained open ground, despite numerous ideas for its redevelopment. The eventual plan, for flats, houses and an office, was completed between 1990 and 1992, to a design by Yeoman McAllister. We now cross the footbridge to the north bank of the Water of Leith.

The area of ground formerly known as the High Green was developed for housing between 1990 and 1992, to designs by Yeoman McAllister. The gable end, and the distinctive chimneys of Hawthorn Buildings, can be seen in the centre of the picture.
Photograph by Jenni Wood.

Well Court, on the north bank of the Water of Leith, was designed by the architect Sydney Mitchell. The development was the idea of John Ritchie Findlay, philanthropic owner of *The Scotsman*, who had it built in 1884 as an experiment in model housing for working people.
Photograph by Jenni Wood.

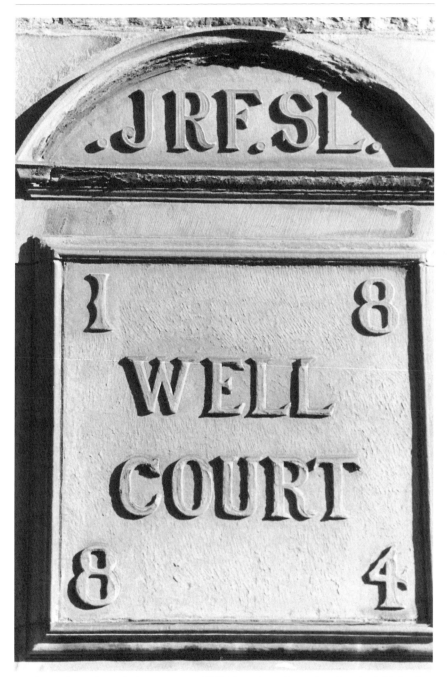

Above the wide-arched entrance to Well Court is a plaque bearing the initials of John Ritchie Findlay and his wife Susan Leslie.
Photograph by Jenni Wood.

The bridge was erected by Tynecastle Ironworks in 1889 beside the old ford, which is still partly visible on the downstream side. On the north side of the bridge, a riverside walkway to Belford Bridge leads off to the left beside a group of flats and houses built on the site of the old tannery of Robert Legget & Sons. Our route continues northwards and turns right into Damside which follows the line of the 'dam' or mill-lade which carried the water from the weir above the village to West Mill. On the south side of Damside a wide-arched entrance leads into Well Court which contains over fifty flats built round a square court-yard, with a separate hall which was used as a club-room for men, and for social functions. Today, Well Court is still mainly residential, but the hall (with the clock-tower) has long been occupied by a firm of architects. The narrow terrace garden, overlooking the Water of Leith, has acquired as an ornament the font from the former Belford Church (built as the second Dean Free Church) which was also designed by Sydney Mitchell. Opposite Well Court is Dean Path Buildings, in sim-ilar style, which was also built for John Ritchie Findlay, but designed by his son, James L. Findlay, who had been a pupil of Sydney Mitchell.

At the east end of Damside our walk divides into a shorter or longer route. The shorter route takes us southwards across Bell's Brae Bridge and back to Kirkbrae House via Belford Road. The longer walk is northwards by Dean Path to see Dean Cemetery, adjacent to the for-mer Dean Orphanage, and back to Belford Road via Belford Bridge and Bell's Mills. The shorter route is described first.

From Damside, cross Bell's Brae Bridge and turn right into Hawthornbank Lane. Instead of following the earlier route, turn left at the big window and go up the flight of steps to Belford Road. The building on the left of the steps is Drumsheugh Baths, which presents a rather squat profile to Belford Road. Designed by John J. Burnet in 1882 with a distinctly Moorish flavour, it exploits fully the steeply falling ground to incorporate three separate floors to Hawthornbank Lane. About £11,000 was spent on acquisition of the site and con-struction of the baths, which were opened on 20th December 1884. The main part of the building, occupied by the swimming pool, consists of a large hall divided into nave and aisles by a series of round-headed arches carried on iron pillars with Moorish capitals.

The vacant ground next to the baths was the site of the first Dean Free Church. The last building on the left in Belford Road has the words Drumsheugh Toll across the front door lintel, below the projecting canopy. The building we see today is not, however, the original tollhouse which stood on the site until the latter years of the nineteenth century. It was replaced in 1891 by the present building which was designed by George Washington Browne as a residence and studio for the artist Charles Martin Hardie R.S.A. Today the ground floor is an office, whilst the upper floor belongs to the Edinburgh Society of Musicians.

We have now completed the shorter walk. The longer walk continues northwards from Damside up the steep slope of Dean Path and past the old tenement building at Convening Court. At the top of Dean Path is the approximate position of the Village of Dean, but nothing remains of it. The old village consisted of one main street with two or three small lanes running off to the east. For the most part the houses were small and single-storeyed with thatched roofs, inhabited mostly by carters and quarrymen at Craigleith Quarry. Its place in political history was assured, however, by the nightly endeavours of the local blacksmith, Robert Orrock, who made pikes to be used by the Friends of the People in their quest for parliamentary reform at the end of the eighteenth century. Their armed uprising was foiled when some of Orrock's pikes were found in the village by two sheriff officers. Several members of the Friends of the People were brought to trial and convicted, apparently on the strength of evidence given by Orrock himself.

The ancient turreted mansion of Dean House lay to the west of the village in extensive grounds, now laid out as Dean Cemetery. This handsome building displayed every conceivable example of Scottish vernacular architecture, with a variety of turrets, corbels and crow-stepped gables. Internally, there was a Great Hall, the ceiling of which was decorated by a series of wooden panels painted in oil and tempera. Seven of these panels, some of which depict biblical scenes, were for long displayed in the former Museum of Antiquities in Queen Street before being rehoused in the new Museum of Scotland in Chambers Street. Dean House was for many generations the seat of the Nisbet family, William Nisbet of Dean, Lord Provost of Edinburgh, being knighted by James VI when he visited Edinburgh in 1617. When the house was demolished in 1845, many of the carved stones were preserved in a wall in Dean Cemetery, and on Kirkbrae House at the south end of Dean Bridge.

One of the seven painted ceiling panels saved from Dean House depicting the
Sacrifice of Isaac, now in the possession of the National Museums of Scotland.
Courtesy of the National Museums of Scotland.

Dean Cemetery was laid out in 1845 to designs by the architect
David Cousin. By the end of the nineteenth century it had become the
'Who's Where' of Edinburgh dignitaries from many walks of life.
Along the west wall are buried several eminent judges of the Court of

Dean Cemetery:

(a) Lieut. John Irving R.N., H.M.S. *Terror*, born 1815, died in King William's Land 1848–9;

(b) Pelicans and winged lions for John Leishman, Writer to the Signet, who died 15th September 1867;

(c) a polished granite pyramid for Lord Rutherfurd, Senator of the College of Justice, who died in 1852;

(d) Sir Thomas Bouch, Civil Engineer, born 25th February 1822, died 30th October 1880, designer of the ill-fated Tay Bridge.

Photographs by Jenni Wood.

Session, including Lords Cowan, Handyside, Cockburn and Jeffrey. Also buried at the Dean are Sir Thomas Bouch, designer of the ill-fated Tay Bridge, John Ritchie Findlay, and the architects William H. Playfair and Robert Reid. From the west side of Dean Cemetery it is possible to see the twin towers of the former Orphan Hospital, rising high above the boundary wall. The 'hospital' was built between 1831 and 1833 from plans drawn by the architect, Thomas Hamilton, who also designed the former Royal High School in Regent Road. In 1995 elaborate plans were announced for the conversion of the Orphan Hospital building to an art gallery, to house the works of the Leith-born sculptor Eduardo Paolozzi, and also temporary exhibitions of modern art. When the plans are fully implemented, it is hoped to construct a gateway between the new gallery and the Dean Cemetery. For the time being, however, there is no direct access from the cemetery to the Orphan Hospital building, nor to the Scottish National Gallery of Modern Art, both of which are reached from Belford Road. We must, therefore, retrace our route a few yards down Dean Path to where there is an opening in the high stone wall with a signpost. A steep flight of steps takes us down to the Water of Leith, the path to the right leading to Belford Bridge. Belford Bridge spans the Water of Leith in one semi-circular stone arch with Edinburgh's Coat of Arms set into panels on the outside face of the parapets. Remaining on the walkway, we go under the bridge and round the back of the Hilton National Hotel (formerly the Dragonara) on the site of Bell's Mills. Adjoining the modern hotel is a three-storey building, originally a granary, with a wheatsheaf and the date, 1807, high on the north wall. A little further up the hill, on the left, is the miller's house dating from c. 1780.

Turning left up Belford Road leads us to the Scottish National Gallery of Modern Art and the Paolozzi gallery. The Gallery of Modern Art can also be reached by following the riverside path upstream for a few hundred yards. However, to complete our Dean Village walk, turn right into Belford Road and cross Belford Bridge. The distinctive red sandstone church (now in secular use) on the corner of Belford Road and Douglas Gardens was built in 1888 as the second Dean Free Church and became Belford Church in 1921. The last section of our walk, on Belford Road, takes us past Sunbury, formerly a largely industrial area. The most important building to survive is

Whytock & Reid's three-storey cabinet works built in 1884. After
Sunbury we pass the new houses on the former High Green, and then
Drumsheugh Baths and Drumsheugh Toll as described in the shorter
walk.

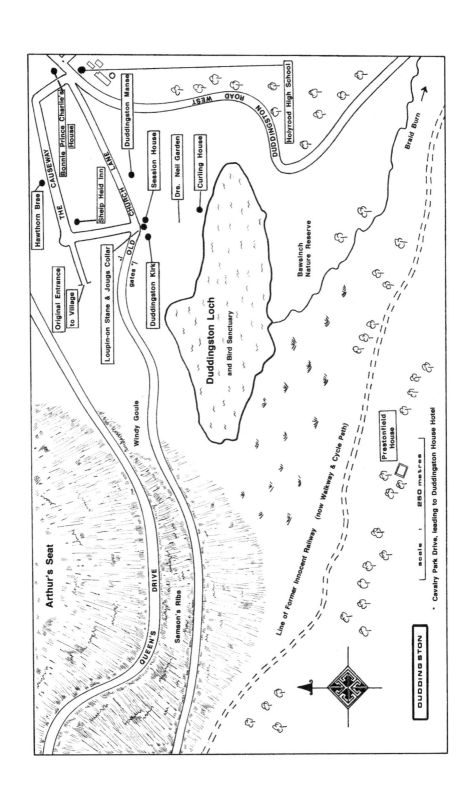

Arthur's Seat

QUEEN'S DRIVE

Samson's Ribs

Windy Goule

Hawthorn Brae

Original Entrance to Village

THE CAUSEWAY

Bonnie Prince Charlie's House

Sheip Heid Inn

Loupin-on Stane & Jougs Collar

OLD CHURCH LANE

gates

Duddingston Kirk

Session House

Duddingston Manse

Drs. Neil Garden

Curling House

DUDDINGSTON ROAD WEST

Holyrood High School

Braid Burn

Duddingston Loch

and Bird Sanctuary

Bawsinch Nature Reserve

Line of Former Innocent Railway (now Walkway & Cycle Path)

Prestonfield House

scale : 250 metres

• Cavalry Park Drive, leading to Duddingston House Hotel

DUDDINGSTON

CHAPTER FIVE

Duddingston

Duddingston village lies in the shelter of Arthur's Seat just outside the eastern boundary of Holyrood Park. The most scenic route from the city centre is to enter the Park at the Palace of Holyroodhouse. Once inside the Park, turn right and follow Queen's Drive uphill to the first roundabout. Continue to the lower roundabout and turn left to take the low road past Samson's Ribs (the rock formation on the left) and the former shepherd's cottage on the right. Within a few hundred yards Duddingston Loch comes into view with the village houses clustered to the left of the old Kirk. The village walk is short with only modest inclines but there is plenty of scope for much longer walks, either along the route of the old Innocent Railway or in Holyrood Park.

Whilst no one would suggest that Duddingston has remained completely unchanged over the years, nevertheless it has been more successful than many other villages in retaining so much of its quiet rural setting. Dating from at least the twelfth century, Duddingston remained, until the early part of the twentieth century, a distinct entity surprisingly uninfluenced by the proximity of the city. It owes its existence to the early church built by the monks of Kelso on the shores of Duddingston Loch around the year 1143. The name Duddingston is derived from Dodin de Berwic (later styled Dodin de Dodinestoun) who obtained a feu of land from Kelso Abbey. With such an ancient history it is hardly surprising that Duddingston has often featured in Scottish history, and in the development of Edinburgh.

This aerial photograph, taken in 1993, shows Duddingston Loch and Duddingston Village in the lower half of the picture. Centre right is Holy Rood High School adjacent to Duddingston Golf Course.
Crown Copyright: Royal Commission on the Ancient and Historical Monuments of Scotland.

THE VILLAGE WALK

It is appropriate that our walk should begin at the most dominant building in the village, namely Duddingston Kirk, believed to be one of the oldest churches in Scotland still in everyday use. It was built on land gifted by David I to the Abbot of Kelso, the feu charters remaining in favour of the Abbot until the Reformation in 1560.

The original church is basically of Norman architecture, although its structure and individual detail have suffered over the years from a variety of causes, not all of which were unavoidable. Fortunately, in recent times, the building has been extensively renovated in keeping with its great antiquity. It is likely that the original church consisted of the nave and chancel only, the square tower with its distinctive parapet of pointed stones having been added much later. It is generally considered, however, that the basic Norman plan was spoiled by the addition, in 1631, of the north transept, built to accommodate the family and tenants of Sir James Hamilton of Prestonfield. The south wall is supported by a series of buttresses surmounted by conical finials (this feature also being repeated on the gables), but the original entrance, also on the south wall and near the tower, has been blocked off. The small Norman windows between the buttresses have also been filled in, the interior of the church now being lit by large stained glass windows. The most significant external feature, dating from Norman times, is the arch over the original doorway, carved in chevron orders. On the left-hand jamb there is a figure of Christ on the cross, and other figures, one of which may be St Peter.

Internally, the only remaining Norman feature is the chancel arch, the outer order of which repeats the chevron design, while the inner order has an angle roll between V-shaped channelling. The position of the pulpit has varied from time to time over the years, sometimes in response to the liturgical requirements of the day. At the time of the Reformation, when the high altar and wrought iron work were removed, a wooden pulpit was erected on the south wall. About 1800 a stone pulpit was built in the corner, on the right-hand side of the chancel arch, and remained in use until 1968 when a new oak pulpit was again built on the south wall. Although there is a most interesting graveyard, a few parishioners have been laid to rest within the church. Within the chancel on the left there is the tomb of Alexander Thomson

Duddingston Village and Loch from Queen's Drive in Holyrood Park.
Photograph by Jenni Wood.

A quiet spot on the banks of Duddingston Loch looking eastwards towards the village, with the distinctive roofline of the kirk in the centre of the skyline.
Photograph by Jenni Wood.

Duddingston Kirk can trace its history to the twelfth century. It is likely that the oldest part of the building is the nave and chancel, with the square tower added later. The ornate stone on the right marks the burial place of David Scot and Margaret Gourley and their eight children. Margaret died on 20th April 1693 aged 48 years.
Photograph by Jenni Wood.

who died on 6th December 1603. The place of burial is marked by a square slab set into the wall, bearing a shield with the arms of the Preston and Thomson families, the initials MATMP and the Latin motto *Dies mortis, aeternae vitae natalis est fidelibus*, translated 'the day of death is for believers the birthday of eternal life'.

The history of Duddingston Kirk is not, however, confined to the church building alone. To the east of the main entrance gate is a curious hexagonal-shaped building of two storeys with lattice windows and a castellated roofline, now known as the Session House. In the early nineteenth century it had a much more sinister use, having been built as a watch tower to combat the lucrative trade in freshly buried corpses. At a time when dwindling numbers were not a problem affecting the living members of the congregation, the elders of the kirk were required, in rotation, to mount guard from the upper storey of the watch tower, to ensure that some poor mortal, just newly buried, was not dug up and

carried off for anatomical research by a gang of hired villains from the
Auld Toon. On the other side of the entrance gate are two equally interesting relics of the past, the loupin-on stane and the jougs collar. The
first of these, a short flight of rough stone steps leading onto a small
square platform, was built at a time when parishioners arrived at church

Rev. John Thomson, distinguished landscape painter and minister at Duddingston
from 1805 to 1840.
From Biographical History of the Scottish People.

on horseback. This simple pile of stones was a source of comfort for old or obese gentlemen, and of modesty for the ladies, as they struggled to mount their horses for the journey back home. The jougs collar was quite another matter: it brought neither comfort nor modesty to anyone. The iron collar and chain, which still hang on the wall, were designed to provide, in one simple session, the time-honoured elements of punishment – retribution, deterrence and reformation. It was used for a wide variety of moral offences including blasphemy, drunkenness, adultery and failure to attend Sunday worship.

Duddingston Manse lies to the east of the Kirk in extensive grounds with a southerly aspect, overlooking the loch and sheltered from the north wind by a high stone wall running the whole length of Old Church Lane. The manse garden is beautifully wooded and leads on, through a small wooden door near the Session House, to a second garden, which runs down to the water's edge. The botanical potential of this previously derelict piece of ground was realised in the 1960s by Dr

At the main entrance to Duddingston Kirk and Kirkyard, the building on the left of the gate is now used as the Session House. It was erected in the early nineteenth century as a watch tower in the days of the resurrectionists. To the right of the gate is the loupin-on stane and the jougs collar.
Photograph by Jenni Wood.

Andrew Neil and his wife Dr Nancy Neil, who have spent a great deal of their time bringing the garden to maturity. It is open to the public on several weekends throughout the year. On more than one occasion recently it has featured in gardening programmes on television. Down at the water's edge is the octagonal-shaped curling house designed in 1823 by William H. Playfair for the Duddingston Curling Society, who made him an honorary member to show their appreciation. The upper floor of the building was used as a studio by Duddingston's most renowned minister, the Rev. John Thomson. It is sometimes said that Thomson, an excellent landscape artist as well as pastor, named the studio 'Edinburgh', thus enabling him, with a clear conscience, to leave a note with his housekeeper explaining that if any parishioner called, she was to say that the minister was not available as he had gone to Edinburgh. The story is dismissed as 'tittle tattle', however, by William Baird, author of *John Thomson of Duddingston*, who maintains that it was the villagers who named the studio 'Edinburgh'.

Our walk round the village begins in The Causeway, directly opposite the entrance gates to the church. Where the road turns sharply to the right, a narrow walled lane comes in from Holyrood Park. This was the original entrance to the village for pedestrians from town, and not 'a short cut to the pub' as suggested by one eminent authority on Edinburgh. It does, however, lead to the ever-popular Sheep Heid Inn, which claims, on its frontage, to have been established in the fourteenth century. In 1845 the parish minister, the Rev. James MacFarlane, though openly tolerating no fewer than four alehouses in the village, insisted in his contribution to the *New Statistical Account of Scotland* that the presence of so many hostelries was justified only on account of the visiting clientèle from Edinburgh. The most famous of these hostelries was the Sheep Heid where 'many opulent citizens resorted in the summer months to solace themselves on one of the ancient homely dishes of Scotland', i.e. sheep heads boiled or baked! It is said that James VI frequented the Sheep Heid, and presented an embellished ram's head and horns, which for many years adorned the bar area. The original silver-mounted ram's head had a small recess to hold snuff, but unfortunately it was lost many years ago and has never been recovered. Although sheep's heads have not been boiled or baked or made into broth there for many years, other interesting traditions survive at the Inn, particularly the old skittle alley to the rear of the premises. Today

The ever-popular Sheep Heid Inn at Duddingston is said to have been frequented by James VI, who presented an embellished ram's head and horns to the proprietor of the day.
Photograph by Jenni Wood.

the Sheep Heid Inn is a homely and welcoming hostelry with cuisine much more varied than would have been available to either James VI or the Rev. MacFarlane.

The remainder of The Causeway contains several interesting nineteenth-century houses, either in private occupation or institutional use. Among these, going from west to east, are : Lochside Cottage, *c.* 1815, with an elegant bow window overlooking the park; Bella Vista, originally built in 1801 and enlarged in 1875; and Hawthorn Brae, a chunky, two-storey building (plus attic and basement) with a splayed staircase leading to a pillared entrance supporting a small balcony. At the east end of The Causeway the road again makes a sharp turn to the right, towards Duddingston Road West. Here on the east side of the road is Duddingston's greatest claim to royal patronage, the short but memorable association with Prince Charles Edward Stuart during his occupation of Edinburgh at the time of the '45 Rebellion. Whilst his troops camped on the flat ground to the east of Duddingston, Bonnie Prince Charlie took up residence in the village on the night before his victory at the Battle of Prestonpans. The two-storey house in The Causeway from which the Prince planned the defeat of General Cope is immortalised in the words of the famous Scottish song:

> Cope sent a challenge frae Dunbar
> Charlie meet me an' ye daur
> And I'll learn you the art o' war
> If you'll meet wi' me in the morning.

Although Prince Charlie's house lay derelict for many years, it has since been restored as private living accommodation, and has a commemorative plaque above the front entrance door.

Holy Rood High School lies to the south-east of Duddingston Road West. It is so close to Duddingston Loch and Bawsinch that flocks of

Prince Charles Edward Stuart took up residence in this house at Duddingston on the night before his victory at the Battle of Prestonpans. The house stands at the east end of The Causeway.
Photograph by Jenni Wood.

Beards, moustaches and watch-chains are very much in evidence in this all-male group from the Trotters Club, photographed in the garden of Duddingston Manse in 1902. In 1909 there were about seventy-three members, many of whom contributed poems and lyrics to the Club's occasional publications.
From The Book of the Trotters Club.

geese mingle with the pupils in the extensive grounds. The school was opened in November 1971 and celebrated its 25th anniversary in 1996. It was created by merging St Anthony's Junior Secondary School in Lochend Road with part of the catchment area of Holy Cross Senior Secondary School in Craighall Road to serve the Catholic community on the east side of the city. In fact it has attracted a cross-denominational roll which has recently risen to 800 from around 450 in the mid-1980s. Children in the first year are drawn, by parental choice, from more than thirty primary schools in Edinburgh. In 1997 there were 53 staff members led by the headteacher, Patrick Sweeney, who was appointed in 1994.

We now turn into Old Church Lane and head back towards the entrance to the church. All along the south side of the road is a high stone wall broken only at the curved entrance to the manse. On the north side of the road are several detached, early nineteenth-century houses, built on feus purchased from the Marquis of Abercorn *c.*1810. The oldest house in the row, though now much altered, probably dates from the eighteenth century. This is Churchhill Cottage which was the village school until 1811 when a new school was built at Duddingston Mills. The schoolmaster continued to live in the house until 1827.

We now proceed past the church gates down the short brae into Holyrood Park where there is a sheltered position on the edge of Duddingston Loch. Most visitors to Duddingston Loch are favourably impressed by its natural tranquillity, especially in an area so close to centres of population. On the other hand, the nineteenth-century historian

This octagonal curling house was designed for the Duddingston Curling Club by
the architect, William H. Playfair. The upper floor of the building, visible above
the rushes, was used as a studio by Duddingston's most renowned minister and
artist, the Rev. John Thomson.
Photograph by Jenni Wood.

William Baird recounts that he once overheard a lady visitor assert that
if the loch were only a little more modest, it would not call itself a loch
at all, but merely a pond. Whether it was that her level of expectation
was too high, or that the level of the water was unexpectedly low, will
never really be known, but at least the position was better than might
have been the case had a civic plan of 1824 been put into effect. The idea
then was to drain the loch completely and pipe the springs to increase
the supply of fresh water needed for Edinburgh. Fortunately for suc-
ceeding generations of curlers, skaters and wildlife enthusiasts the plan
was never implemented.

Although curling existed at Duddingston before 1795, it was not

The Lord High Steward dressed and equipped for the roarin' game at Duddingston. *From* The Book of the Trotters Club.

until that year that a proper club was formed, the Duddingston Curling Society, with rules and regulations to govern its affairs. The Society still exists but it is many years since it played at Duddingston. In the early days, the Society consisted mainly of local men, but by 1800 it had begun to attract several members from Edinburgh, one of whom, James Millar, Advocate, assisted in establishing the first rules of the game. He was responsible for the Latin motto adopted by the Society: *Sic Scoti: alii non aeque felices* – This is the way the Scots play: the rest of the world isn't half so lucky. The Society grew in strength and influence, special badges being struck in 1802 bearing the motto, and depicting curlers on the ice at Duddingston with Duddingston Kirk in the background, and on the reverse side the inscription 'Duddingston Curling Society Instituted 17th January 1795'. A code of curling laws devised and approved by the Society on 6th January 1804 was incorporated in the Lochmaben Curling Society rules in 1829, and contributed substantially to the first rules of the Grand Caledonian Curling Club. By 1823 the old curling house at Duddingston was in very poor condition, and this led to the construction of a new stone one, designed by the architect William H. Playfair. This is the octagonal tower which can be seen across the loch, the upper storey of which was used by the Rev. John Thomson as his 'Edinburgh' studio. The lower storey, at water level, was used as the curling house. Several illustrations show the surface of Duddingston Loch frozen over, and the whole arena given over to curling, skating and other pastimes. In fact, much of the curling was done on artificially constructed, shallow ponds on the south side of the loch, which froze over more quickly and were much safer in the event of the ice cracking. These ponds still exist, covered in vegetation, but they cannot be reached in safety.

As we look out over the loch it is not difficult to imagine it as the home of curling but it is much more difficult to see it as it might have been in the eighth century B.C. In 1796 the *Old Statistical Account of Scotland* drew attention to the fact that an interesting find of Roman spears and javelins had been made at Duddingston Loch a few years previously. The discovery was actually made in 1778 by workmen dredging for marl in the loch, and although the weapons were long believed to be of Roman origin, advances in archaeological expertise since then have shown that the artefacts date from the Late Bronze Age. At the time of the find, the loch was owned by Sir Alexander Dick, who was sufficiently public-spirited to make a gift in 1781 of most of the items to the embryonic Museum of the Society of Antiquaries of Scotland (later the National Museum of Antiquities of Scotland and now the Royal Museum of Scotland). These were the first objects to be given to the Society, which was founded in 1780 by David, 11th Earl of Buchan. Among the items found at Duddingston were a ring from a cauldron and parts of swords, daggers and spearheads.

Today the reedy waters of the loch are the natural habitat of a wide variety of fish, wildfowl and other birds. It was not until 1925, however, that the area was officially designated Duddingston Bird Sanctuary, after the loch and its environs had been gifted to the nation by William Haggerston Askew of Ladykirk. The loch and the Sanctuary come under the administration of Historic Scotland, who work in close liaison with the Scottish Wildlife Trust in matters of everyday management. Since 1925 a great many species of birds have been recorded including the bittern in 1955, the peregrine falcon in 1956, and the golden oriole in 1978; in the winters from 1993 to 1996 the bittern have again returned. A heronry has been formed of about a dozen nests since inlets were excavated in the reeds in 1985. By far the most spectacular visitors were, however, the 8,000-strong flock of pochard which roosted on the loch during the winter months before flying off to Scandinavia and Russia for the summer. Their habit of roosting on the loch at Duddingston by day and feeding on the Forth by night continued until 1976 when the City built the Seafield Sewage Works which deprived the birds of the nutrients of a rich feeding ground. There is also a resident flock of greylag geese, started in 1961 with only thirteen birds, and now totalling about 370, but kept in check by foxes and mink.

To the south (the opposite side of the loch to our vantage point) there is a triangular piece of ground known as Bawsinch which lay waste for many years until a housing development was proposed in 1969. This unbelievably insensitive proposal was fortunately abandoned and in 1971 the ground was bought by the Scottish Wildlife Trust for £10,000 to create Bawsinch Nature Reserve. Although the primary object of acquiring the ground was to provide a buffer zone for Duddingston Bird Sanctuary, it was soon obvious that Bawsinch had great potential in providing an additional habitat for a wide variety of wildlife. After the land was cleared, planting was done in natural groups to include all the trees and shrubs native to Scotland and other parts of Britain. To extend the variety of habitat, artificial ponds were dug and named Matthew, Mark, Luke and John. More recent ponds have been constructed called Carse, Duckscrape, Rock Trap and Volunteer. A number of additional projects have reached fruition in recent years. These include: the Gunn Loch (created from a bequest by Peter Gunn of the Edinburgh Natural History Society); Goose Green, which provides ideal grazing for greylag geese, mallard, partridge and pheasant; and the Connell Hide skilfully camouflaged to allow ornithologists to study the wildlife on the loch and in the reedbeds nearby. The reedbed has also had three kilometers of inlet excavated in it as extra edge-habitat for birds and fish breeding grounds. A sand-face has been constructed in the hope of attracting sand martins to breed. There is no automatic public access to Bawsinch or the Bird Sanctuary but interested parties can apply to the Scottish Wildlife Trust, Cramond House, Kirk Cramond.

There is one last topic in the Duddingston story. It entails a slightly longer walk around the south side of the loch by way of the Innocent Railway line, now reconstructed as a walkway and cycle path. From the north side of the loch take the road uphill through Windy Goule and past Samson's Ribs. This section of the road has a good view out over Prestonfield Golf Course and Prestonfield House to the hills of Blackford, Braid and Pentland. At Samson's Ribs the walkway begins near the old tunnel where the line came down from St Leonard's. Follow the walkway eastwards (with the Golf Course on your right) until it emerges at Duddingston Road West. Turning left at Duddingston Road West leads back to Old Church Lane in Duddingston village.

The Innocent Railway, built and designed by one of Edinburgh's most famous civil engineers, James Jardine, was opened in July 1831, primarily to carry coal from the pits around Dalkeith to the goods yard at St Leonard's in the Pleasance. As it was the first railway ever built in Edinburgh, technology was in its infancy, so much so that the Edinburgh & Dalkeith Railway Company, incorporated in 1826 to run the service, did not actually possess any trains. The motive power was the humble horse. As the Company prospered, branch lines were extended to Fisherrow and Leith, until by 1840 the annual volume of traffic was 300,000 passengers and 120,000 tons of freight. After the initial exertion of getting the rolling stock to move out of the station at St Leonard's, the horses had a fairly easy section of about 200 yards to the head of the tunnel. They did not enter the tunnel but were uncoupled and led to the other end, ready to continue the journey. As the gradient inside the tunnel was very steep, an ingenious system was adopted of counter-balancing a down train with an up train, linked to two 25 h.p. static steam engines which did the hauling from the top of the tunnel. Once out of the tunnel, the train was safely on the meandering track to Duddingston and all stations east. It was this idyllic

The Innocent Railway was designed and built by the civil engineer, James Jardine, and was opened in July 1831. It carried passengers and freight from St Leonard's in the Pleasance to Dalkeith. The Duddingston section of the route is now the Innocent Cycleway and Footpath. The photograph shows a short section of the track near Duddingston Road West.
Crown Copyright: Royal Commission on the Ancient and Historical Monuments of Scotland.

setting, and its excellent safety record, which inspired Dr Robert Chambers to refer to the innocence of the railway, an expression which eventually gave rise to its name. By 1844 the North British Railway Company had been formed, and in the following year it acquired the Innocent Railway. The old gauge of 4′ 6″ was replaced by the new standard gauge, paving the way for more than a century of service using steam power. After closure of the line in 1968, little use was made of it

Duddingston
House, to the east
of Duddingston
Road West, was
built between
1763 and 1768 for
James, 8th Earl of
Abercorn, to
designs by the
architect, Sir
William
Chambers. The
house is presently
occupied by the
architects, Percy
Johnson-Marshall
& Partners.
*Courtesy of Percy
Johnson-Marshall
& Partners.*

until 1981 (150 years after its official opening) when work was commenced on the construction of the Innocent Cycleway/Footpath, opened on 16th August 1982 by Mrs Lynda Chalker M.P., then Parliamentary Under-Secretary of State for Transport.

Two important houses can be seen from the line of the Innocent Railway, depending upon the amount of foliage on the trees. To the right (southwards) is Prestonfield House surrounded by trees adjacent to Prestonfield Golf Course. Prestonfield House was built in the 1680s for Sir James Dick, Lord Provost of Edinburgh, to replace an earlier house destroyed by fire. It is now used as a hotel with an entrance driveway from Priestfield Road.

The second house is Duddingston House which can be seen almost directly in line with the walkway. It lies to the east of Duddingston Road West and is approached either from a short road along the side of Holy Rood High School or from entrance gates on Milton Road West. Duddingston House was built between 1763 and 1768 for James, eighth Earl of Abercorn, to designs by the architect Sir William Chambers. Chambers was responsible for the design of several well-known buildings, notably the town house of Sir Lawrence Dundas in St Andrew Square, Edinburgh, in 1771 (now occupied by the Royal Bank of Scotland), and Somerset House in London in 1772. Much of the original grounds of Duddingston House survives as Duddingston Golf Course. The house is presently occupied by the architects, Percy Johnson-Marshall & Partners, who have been responsible for the renovation and restoration of many of the original features. It is two storeys in height with a grand pedimented portico supported by four Corinthian columns. The front entrance door leads into a beautifully proportioned hall taking the height of both storeys. The principal rooms are entered from the hall and there is a central staircase leading to the upper floor. The pedimented stable block to the north and the corresponding kitchen block to the south have been converted to private living accommodation.

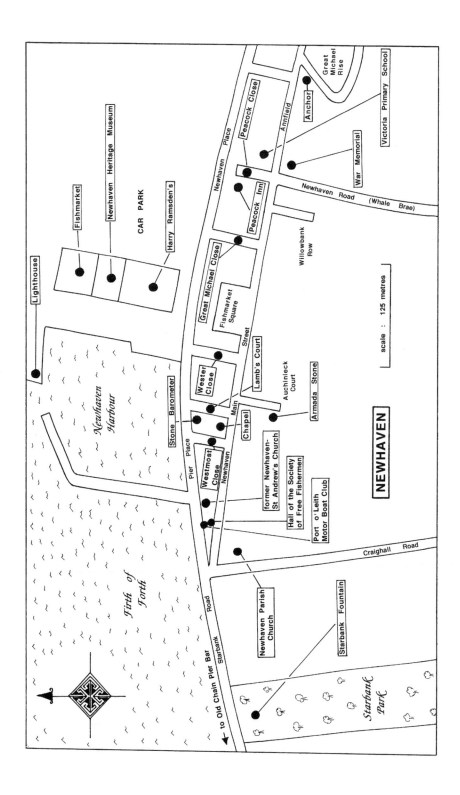

NEWHAVEN

scale : 125 metres

Firth of Forth

Newhaven Harbour

to Old Chain Pier Bar

Lighthouse

Fishmarket

Newhaven Heritage Museum

CAR PARK

Harry Ramsden's

Stone Barometer

Wester Close

Westmost Close

Pier Place

Newhaven

Main Street

Chapel

former Newhaven-
St Andrew's Church

Hall of the Society
of Free Fishermen

Port o'Leith
Motor Boat Club

Great Michael Close

Fishmarket Square

Lamb's Court

Auchinleck Court

Armada Stone

Newhaven Place

Peacock Close

Peacock Inn

Anchor

Annfield

Great Michael Rise

Victoria Primary School

War Memorial

Newhaven Road (Whale Brae)

Willowbank Row

Craighall Road

Newhaven Parish Church

Starbank Road

Starbank Fountain

Starbank Park

CHAPTER SIX

Newhaven

Newhaven is one of Edinburgh's coastal villages, lying almost equidistant from Granton Harbour in the west and Leith Docks in the east. Its early history was consistent with its becoming Edinburgh's premier port, but, in fact, it was usurped, firstly by Leith, and then, at a much later date, by Granton. New Haven came to prominence in the early sixteenth century in opposition to the old haven of Blackness further up the Forth. Known at one time as Our Lady's Port of Grace, Newhaven saw the construction and launching of the *Great Michael*, the largest warship of its time and the envy of almost every seafaring nation in the world. Unfortunately, the natural deepwater channels around the old harbour were never fully exploited, and a proposed ship canal linking Newhaven and Leith never got past the drawing board.

Newhaven established itself as a close-knit fishing community in which social convention dictated that young men and women should not marry people from outside the village. The confusion caused by the recurrence of the same surnames was avoided by introducing by-names: thus Sandy Rutherford was known as Sandy Whitestar, the by-name being taken from the name of his father's fishing boat.

At the present day the fishing industry has all but gone; the fishwives no longer carry their creels in the streets of Edinburgh; and many of the old houses have been demolished and rebuilt. The cycle has been broken. As newcomers establish their own way of life, the old order remains only in the minds of the older inhabitants. Although the village has been integrated with Edinburgh for many years, its physical form is still very evident, and there are several places of historical interest for the enquiring visitor. The village walk is compact, the terrain is mostly level, and there are several comfortable hostelries affording protection from the east wind.

An aerial view of Newhaven Harbour and the village in the 1970s, after the south side of Main Street had been rebuilt. The herring fleet has gone from the harbour but the fish market, to the left of the picture, is still operational. Part of it is now occupied as Harry Ramsden's Fish Restaurant, and the Newhaven Heritage Museum.

Courtesy of The Scotsman Publications Ltd.

THE VILLAGE WALK

From Pier Place, looking out over the harbour, dotted with all manner of pleasure craft, it is difficult to imagine that within living memory this small haven supported a vibrant fishing industry with its own market and deep-freeze facilities. Several centuries earlier it was chosen by James IV as the Royal Dockyards from which the *Great Michael* was launched in 1511, under the command of Sir Andrew Wood. Andrew Wood was born in the middle of the fifteenth century in Largo, Fife and spent the early part of his life as a merchant and skipper operating out of the port of Leith. He was the proud owner of two ships, the *Flower* and the *Yellow Carvel*, each of 300 tons burden, which he used to build up significant trade routes with the Low Countries. His resilience, and skill in navigation, did not go unnoticed. James III granted him a lease of the lands of Largo on condition that he kept the *Yellow Carvel* in constant repair for the use of the King whenever required. In 1483 he obtained a grant of ownership of the land, and shortly thereafter he was knighted. Rapid rise to fame on account of naval ability was of great interest to other monarchs. Henry VII was clearly unhappy at the growing supremacy of Sir Andrew's fleet and issued a challenge to any of his subjects who would engage and defeat the impertinent Scot. Stephen Bull took up the challenge in 1489 and lay in wait for Sir Andrew in the shelter of the Isle of May. As Sir Andrew rounded St Abb's Head and saw the English vessels blocking his route home, he made hurried preparation for battle. The ensuing struggle was long and bloody but Sir Andrew emerged victorious. It is little wonder, therefore, that Sir Andrew was chosen to command the *Great Michael* when it was launched as the flagship of the Scottish navy. Designed by the famous naval architect, Jacques Tarette, and costing £30,000, it required for its construction almost all the oak in Fife. It was 240 feet long, 36 feet wide, and carried three hundred sailors, one hundred and twenty gunners and one thousand troops. Its fighting ability, however, never matched that of the much lighter and smaller *Yellow Carvel*. Indeed it was so big and cumbersome that it never successfully led the Scottish navy into any major conflict. With the death of James IV at Flodden in 1513, hopes of a successful navy evaporated, and the *Great Michael* was sold to France, allegedly for 40,000 livres.

Equal fame never returned but three centuries later Newhaven had a second chance to be 'among the first commercial ports of the Empire'. Such were the aspirations of James Anderson, civil engineer, whose *Report on the Present State of Leith Harbour* was published by Adam and Charles Black of Edinburgh in 1834. On the basis of many years' study of the tides, currents and winds along the coastline, Anderson had come to the conclusion that Leith would never be anything other than a tidal harbour, hampered by shifting sandbanks at its entrance, and continually fouled by alluvial deposits from the Water of Leith. Anderson's remedy was simple. Leith had better facilities on land, and Newhaven had the advantage of a natural deepwater channel out into the Forth estuary. He proposed to form a new entrance at Newhaven and to construct a ship canal running east to the docks at Leith. The canal was to be 200 feet wide with a stone quay along its entire length, protected at the Newhaven end by flood gates and substantial sea defences. It was a most ambitious and far-reaching plan, costed by Anderson at £124,695, who added the cautionary warning that if it was not taken up by those who commissioned him, an alternative scheme would be adopted by their competitors. His worst fears were confirmed. Anderson's plan was rejected, and within ten years a second pier had been opened at Granton. Newhaven settled for improvements to the sea walls in 1837; a breakwater by Robert Stevenson in 1864; and a complete reconstruction, with the addition of a lighthouse, between 1876 and 1881.

Despite losing the advantage of the link to Leith, Newhaven built up significant trade routes for freight and passengers. The steamer *Tourist* plied between Newhaven and Aberdeen, and there was also regular passage to and from Kirkcaldy, Burntisland and Pettycur. One of the longer sea routes was from London to Newhaven, which took about three days depending upon the weather and the time of year. On 7th July 1832 the steamship *James Watt* left London for the journey north, with Sir Walter Scott on board, returning from Italy. Sir Walter was desperately ill and remained unconscious even after the vessel berthed at Newhaven on 9th July. Still unaware of his surroundings, he was driven to the Douglas Hotel in St Andrew Square, Edinburgh, where he rested for the following two days. He then made his last journey to Abbotsford, where he died on 21st September 1832, worn out by his prodigious efforts to clear his earlier debts.

Morning Star II, part of the former herring fleet, at the quayside at Newhaven
Harbour, *c.* 1964.
Courtesy of The Scotsman Publications Ltd.

Newhaven harbour was for many years the centre of a busy fishing
industry until its gradual decline in the 1950s. Like most other fishing
villages in Scotland, there was hardly a single family in Newhaven
which did not have some connection with the industry. Fathers and
sons went to sea; mothers and daughters helped with the nets and lines;
and intermarriage in the village ensured that young wives had, at least,
a basic training in the harsh realities of a fisherman's family. Many of
the womenfolk also worked as fishwives selling fish direct to house-
wives in most districts of Edinburgh and beyond.

The date 1793 is traditionally given as the year in which herring were
discovered in the Firth of Forth. James Colston, author of *The Town
and Port of Leith*, writing in 1892, relates the story of how 'this fertile

source of revenue' was discovered accidentally by Thomas Brown of
Donibristle when he was fishing one day with hook and line. The herring were so plentiful then that they could be gathered in bucketfuls:

>Wha'll buy my caller herrin'?
>They're bonny fish and halesome farin';
>Wha'll buy my caller herrin'?
>New drawn frae the Forth.

There was, of course, a darker side to the business of catching fish,
when men and boys risked their lives to land a catch in atrocious
weather conditions:

>Wha'll buy my caller herrin'?
>They're no brought here without brave darin',
>Buy my caller herrin',
>Ye little ken their worth.

>Wha'll buy my caller herrin'?
>O Ye may ca' them vulgar farin';
>Wives and mithers, maist despairin',
>Ca' them lives o' men.

The other great source of revenue was the oyster beds, harvested
amidst almost constant controversy from the sixteenth century.
Edinburgh always maintained that it owned what was generally known
as the City Scalps, yet the men of Newhaven depended upon them for
a decent living. Many attempts were made during the seventeenth and
eighteenth centuries to regulate the conflicting interests of the industry,
but without much success. Amid great acrimony the case came before
the High Court of Admiralty from 1791 to 1793. For the Newhaven
men the court's decision in their favour was something of a Pyrrhic victory. Whilst the court affirmed that boats from Prestonpans and
Cockenzie had no rights to the oysters, it re-established Edinburgh's
claim to ownership, with the important rider that it could be exercised
only through the Society of Free Fishermen of Newhaven. By 1866 the
fleet was almost one hundred boats but over-fishing and bad management eventually led the industry into a decline from which it did not
recover. When other fish were plentiful and the price relatively stable,
the Dock Commissioners invested £20,000 in the erection of a new fish
market on the east side of the harbour, which was opened on 5th

Pleasure craft only at Newhaven Harbour in 1996. In the background is Pier Place, with the former St Andrew's Free Church, now used by Alien Rock for indoor rock climbing.
Photograph by Jenni Wood.

December 1896. By 1932, 16,000 cwts of herring were landed annually
and processed at Newhaven market along with a much larger quantity
of halibut, plaice, hake, cod and haddock. Although new quick-freez-
ing plant was installed in the early 1950s, by then the Newhaven fleet
was in serious decline. At the present day there are occasional working
boats out of Newhaven Harbour, but there is no fleet as such: only the
fish market remains.

Despite the loss of the fleet, and the bustle which took place on the
quayside, the village of Newhaven still looks like a Scottish fishing
community and retains many physical links with its former lifestyle.
Beginning at Pier Place, beside the harbour, the most dominant landmark is the spire of the former St Andrew's Free Church, built in 1852
to designs by the architect F. Anderson Hamilton. The halls and the
steeple were not added until 1883. The Free Church congregation was
established by the Rev. James Fairbairn who 'came out' from
Newhaven Parish Church, along with a substantial following from the
congregation, at the Disruption in 1843. Fairbairn was a man who
understood the fisherfolk around him and was able to identify with
their needs and their thoughts, especially at times when men were lost

The Newhaven float, with local women in traditional gala dress, took second
prize at the Edinburgh Royal Infirmary Pageant on 28th May 1927. The lorry was
lent for the occasion by David Dryburgh, the trawler owner, from Granton.
Courtesy of Newhaven Heritage Museum.

Rev. James Fairbairn, the first Disruption minister of St Andrew's Free Church, immortalised as the caring cleric by Charles Reade in his novel, *Christie Johnstone*.
From Grant's Old and New Edinburgh.

at sea. His spiritual comfort was matched by his practical ingenuity. At a time when the fishing fleet was lacking in prosperity and direction the Rev. James Fairbairn led a campaign for the rebuilding and modernisation of the entire fleet, consisting of thirty-three large boats, each requiring an expenditure of £250, a sum utterly beyond the financial resources of families in a small fishing community. He died in 1879, leader of a very loyal congregation, and immortalised by Charles Reade as the caring cleric in his novel *Christie Johnstone*. St Andrew's became a United Free Church in 1900 and was renamed Newhaven-St Andrew's at the union with the established church in 1929. In 1974 Newhaven-St Andrew's entered into a union with Newhaven on Forth to form Newhaven Parish Church in Craighall Road, after which the old St Andrew's Free Church building was sold for secular use.

A few yards east of the church building, near Lamb's Court, there is a tall stone barometer case first erected in 1775, then re-erected in 1900 with a ship cut into a square moulding, and round the base the words, SOCIETY OF FREE FISHERMEN. The adjacent stone-fronted tenement, with the clock in the pediment, was also erected by the Society. Further east again is one of Newhaven's oldest hostelries, the Peacock Inn. The traditions of its first owner, Mr Peacock, are proudly maintained by the present proprietors who come from an old-established Newhaven family. Originally, the Peacock consisted of a few one-storey cottages facing the sea, but later a more substantial square building was erected in Peacock's Court with bar accommodation on the ground floor, and the dining room and bedrooms on the upper floor. The present accommodation is to the west of Peacock Court, refurbished in a style which befits an old fishing village. A fireplace has recently been restored showing a magnificient peacock in coloured tiles, and there are numerous artefacts pertaining to boats and the fishing industry. Among these are a model of the *Great Michael*, large dolls wearing traditional dress of the Newhaven fishwife, and a set of photographs by David Octavius Hill and Robert Adamson showing life in Newhaven around 1844.

Newhaven has recently acquired another interesting venue specialising in fish dishes. In part of the old fish market to the east of the quayside is Harry Ramsden's Fish Restaurant which came to Newhaven in 1993. Harry Ramsden opened his first fish and chip shop in 1928 in Guiseley, Yorkshire in a small wooden hut which was

The south-facing frontage of the old Peacock Hotel which belonged to Mrs Main, daughter and successor to the late Mrs Clark. The present-day Peacock Inn is in adjacent premises facing the harbour.

bought for £150. As trade improved he moved to bigger premises in 1932 and continued to expand the business throughout the country and abroad. There are now twenty outlets, two of which are in Scotland, the first being in Glasgow in 1991.

The Newhaven Heritage Museum is located in the middle section of the old fish market, and was opened on 25th May 1994 by Nelly Walls, the oldest surviving fishwife from Newhaven. The idea of the Heritage Museum is part of a broader vision of a network of community museums throughout the city. At Newhaven part of that vision became a reality when Edinburgh District Council was offered a twenty-year free lease of the building from Edinburgh Fish Restaurants Ltd., which was proposing to establish a Harry Ramsden's Fish Restaurant in part of the old fish market. LEEL (Lothian and Edinburgh Enterprise Limited)

Harry Ramsden, the uncrowned king of fish and chips, first established his
business in Guiseley, Yorkshire in 1928.
Courtesy of Harry Ramsden's.

Harry Ramsden's Fish Restaurant (right), a popular venue for all ages, includes
alfresco meals on the quayside.
Photograph by Jenni Wood.

assisted with funding for setting up the displays. Many of the exhibits were donated from private individuals with an interest in Newhaven or actively collected by Museum staff. Other items were lent by the Scottish Record Office, Trinity House and the National Museums of Scotland. In its first complete year (1995) the annual admissions at Newhaven totalled over 33,000. The Museum is administered by the City of Edinburgh Council; and a team of dedicated volunteers, with strong Newhaven connections, are on hand to assist visitors by answering questions and helping them with the displays. The exhibits cover every aspect of the old village of Newhaven and its long association with fishing. There are separate sections on the Society of Free Fishermen, the churches, the choirs, Victoria School and the Gala Days. Of particular interest is the array of fish boxes, creels and tools, and instruction on knot-tying and net-making. Visitors are also allowed to dress up in the old fishwives' costumes donated by Newhaven families. The individual exhibits include a large-scale model of the *Great Michael* by George Scammell and a bronze of Mistress Esther Liston, Fishwife of Newhaven, by the sculptor Julian Allan (1892–1996).

Returning to the south side of Pier Place, we pass the rear of Victoria Primary School and turn right into Annfield. According to *The Place Names of Edinburgh* by Stuart Harris, the name Annfield 'is recorded from 1763, when the land's owner John Steuart of Blairhaw, whose wife's name was Ann, began to style himself "of Annfield"'. At its east end the long terrace of three-storey houses was begun around 1806 but was not finished until nearly fifty years later. Beside the big anchor fixed to the pavement, there are modern flats constructed at ground-floor level of setts taken from the old village street. To the west are red sandstone tenements built in the 1930s on the site of Fishermen's Park. Newhaven's War Memorial, to the memory of the men of the Newhaven churches who fell in the Great War 1914–1918, is set into the face of the tenement on the corner of Annfield and Newhaven Road. The fading inscriptions include the names of the men who belonged to the Parish Church and the Free Church, followed by the words 'Erected by John Pottinger 1935'. Immediately opposite, Victoria Primary School boldly portrays the words '1843 Leith School Board 1885' below which is the corresponding War Memorial to the men and women of Newhaven who fell in the Second World War 1939–1945.

A poignant moment as the womenfolk of Newhaven lay a wreath at the village War Memorial *c*. 1937.
Courtesy of Newhaven Heritage Museum.

A happier moment as the womenfolk of Newhaven assemble for the annual picnic, photographed in New Lane, with the bus driver, and an accordionist to accompany the singing.
Courtesy of Newhaven Heritage Museum.

It was unveiled on 6th June 1948 by the Lady Provost, Rodney Margaret Murray, sister of the Lord Provost, Sir Andrew Murray, who was also present.

Newhaven can trace the history of its schools to the early eighteenth century when the first recorded building was in School Close or Lamb's Court, off Main Street. No records survive but it is generally supposed that it was administered by the Society of Free Fishermen. In 1844 Dr James Buchanan of North Leith Church headed a committee to find a feu of ground for the first Victoria School building. When the school was taken over by Leith School Board in 1874, the number of places

Main Street and Annfield showing the entrance to Peacock Court, beyond which is Victoria Primary School. On the left is one of Newhaven's old hostelries, the Bow Tow.
Photograph by Jenni Wood.

was one hundred and fifty. The earliest log books have not survived but an entry in September 1875 states that it was necessary for the Infant Department to meet in the old Free Fishermen's School because the new part of Victoria School was not quite ready for the pupils. Additional accommodation was added to the school in 1884, 1897 and 1930. Newhaven's proximity to the Forth and to Leith Docks meant that 1939 was a time of great apprehension for everyone in the village. On 2nd September 1939 many pupils and parents were evacuated to Fort William, and arrangements were made for teaching the remaining pupils in various private houses. Despite, or perhaps because of, the increased workload involving air raid shelter practices, gas mask drill, fire watching and numerous alerts, the headmaster was able to record on 30th June 1944 a memorable centenary session. On 30th October 1944 a copy of the Newhaven 'Armada' stone, presented by Henry Robb, Shipbuilders, was unveiled by the Lord Provost, Sir William Y. Darling, to mark the centenary of the school. The carved wooden plaque is an exact copy of the original stone which can still be seen in the village at Auchinleck Court. At the centenary service pupils of the school were dressed in traditional Newhaven costume: the girls wore striped petticoats and shawls, and the boys wore blue home-knitted jerseys. Ernest Brown, M.P., reminded the children that on the platform there were representatives of the three things that Hitler hated most – the Church, Parliament and Education. Happier days returned on 8th May 1945 when Victory in Europe was declared over the radio and the school closed for two days' holiday. In the post-war years Victoria School served its population well, and at the present time is acutely aware of its responsibilities to keep alive the old traditions of Newhaven. The school maintains a small museum of old photographs of the village. old street signs, model ships, creels and nets.

We now leave Victoria Primary School and proceed westwards along the old main street of the village. Traffic restrictions introduced some years ago have produced a double effect: the roadway is devoid of fast-flowing through traffic but the centre of activity has been moved away from Main Street. In the 1970s almost £2 million was spent on the complete demolition and re-building of the south side of Main Street, and the refurbishment of many of the properties and closes on the north side. Three-storey flats were designed for the south side by Ian G. Lindsay & Partners, who took the trouble to

Reliance, the last boat made at Newhaven, and built at Allan & Brown's yard, Fishermen's Park, 1929, is hauled through the streets to the harbour. *Courtesy of the late Peter Carnie.*

incorporate the ancient Newhaven 'Armada' stone in the gable wall of No. 6 Auchinleck Court. This stone has a most interesting history, recorded in the *Inventory of the Ancient and Historical Monuments of the City of Edinburgh* (1951). It has been moved on more than one occasion in the past. It consists of two carved panels which were built into the front of Newhaven Post Office, Main Street in 1914, after having been saved from an old cottage which stood previously on the same site. The upper triangular panel has a thistle on the top, the inscription NEMO ME IMPUNI (*sic*) LACESSET (let no one provoke me with impunity), the date 1588, and the words IN THE NEAM OF GOD. Between the date and the inscription there is a rigged ship with flags on all three masts displaying the St Andrew's Cross. The lower square panel has a seventeenth-century moulding containing two globes in the lower part and a sextant, anchor and cross-staff in

The Newhaven 'Armada' stone, dated 1588, is incorporated in the gable end of Auchinleck Court. This photograph shows it at a previous location in the old Main Street, c. 1909.

the upper part. This is the stone which is reproduced at Victoria Primary School.

Fishmarket Square opens out from the north side of Main Street and communicates with Pier Place. The square was previously known as St Andrew's Square but the name was changed in 1968 to avoid confusion with the similar name, St Andrew Square, in the New Town of Edinburgh. To the west of Fishmarket Square three old closes have been retained, Wester Close, Lamb's Court and Westmost Close. Between Lamb's Court and Westmost Close there is a small area of ground with a perimeter railing protecting what remains of Newhaven's oldest building. This is the ancient Chapel of St Mary and St James, built around 1508 by James IV as a place of worship for the shipwrights who worked on the *Great Michael*. The chapel gradually fell into disuse, particularly after the Siege of Leith in 1544 and the Reformation in 1560. By 1611 it was reported as being in ruins. The site was acquired by the Society of Free Fishermen in the middle of the eighteenth century and used by them as a place of burial until 1848. There is an interesting footnote in Alexander Campbell's *History of Leith* (1827) which states that an elegantly cut ornamental model of a cannon in stone, and a holy water font belonging to the ancient chapel, were in the possession of a gentleman living near Newhaven. Unfortunately no trace of these items has been found in recent years, but in 1972 a most important archaeological dig was undertaken at the chapel under the direction of the Department of Educational Studies at Edinburgh University. Several trenches were dug which revealed a mass of human skeletons in disarray, suggesting that they had been moved from some other area. At greater depths more skeletons were found, but in more ordered positions. Some skeletal remains were enclosed in wooden coffins, and the bodies were wrapped in shrouds. The team was also successful in locating the foundations of the outer walls, which suggested a rectangular building, measuring internally approximately sixty-three by twenty-one feet. There were some traces of facing mortar on the inside, but there was no flooring apart from a few slabs, and there was no sign of an altar or other fitments. Small artefacts, found on the site, include medieval pottery, clay tobacco pipes and a twopenny piece of the reign of Charles I, minted in 1632. At the present day the most complete part of the chapel is the west gable which contains a rectangular seventeenth-century window.

To the west of the old chapel, the building with crow-stepped stonework above the upper windows was built in 1877 as the Hall of the Society of Free Fishermen of Newhaven. The Hall was opened at a grand soirée on Friday 18th January 1878, the leading dignitaries being Baillie Colston, the City Chamberlain, and the Rev. James Fairbairn. Almost from time immemorial the affairs of the fishing industry, and the provision of social benefits to the old and infirm people of Newhaven, were in the hands of the Society of Free Fishermen. Tradition has it that the Society dates from the fifteenth century but it was not until 1631 that meetings became more formal and records were kept. Prior to 1817 membership was open to anyone, but when the Society grew to unmanageable proportions, a rule was passed confining membership to 'the lawful sons of fishermen whose names were clear on the books'. In its early years the Society's involvement in the community was almost equivalent to that of a small town council, with responsibility for welfare, burials, collection of fish tithes and control

A horse bus and an open-topped electric car at the foot of Craighall Road, 1912.

Newhaven Parish Church, in Craighall Road, was designed by the architect John Henderson, and opened on 30th October 1836.
Photograph by Jenni Wood.

of the oyster beds. In recent years the hall has been acquired by the Port o' Leith Motor Boat Club who have maintained the old traditions by remodelling the interior to resemble the *Great Michael* warship.

At the foot of Craighall Road the village street ends abruptly with a

The Old Chain Pier Bar, in Trinity Crescent, takes its name from the Old Chain Pier which was destroyed in a violent storm on 18th October 1898.
Photograph by Jenni Wood.

pavement and railing blocking vehicular access, but providing a useful site for the commemorative seat, presented by Charles Addison to mark the Golden Jubilee, 1927–1977, of the Newhaven Fisherwomen's Choir. West of Main Street there are several other strong historical ties with the old village.

A few yards into Craighall Road, on the left, is Newhaven Parish Church dating from 1836. The first minister was the Rev. James Fairbairn, already referred to, who joined the Free Church in 1843. Such was Fairbairn's personal following in Newhaven that the parish church suffered greatly by his departure, and did not really begin to recover until the appointment of the Rev. William Graham in 1859. In 1870 Craighall Road was opened up and the front of the church was enclosed with railings. Attractive as they were, they appear to have provided scant comfort for the Trustees, who expressed 'great regret that such a roadway past the Church should exist at all'. On the appointment of the Rev. Thomas Pearson in 1887, the church entered a long period of prosperity and influence. The new minister was a man of considerable musical ability who was keen to appoint an organist of a sufficiently high calibre to do justice to the new organ installed a few years earlier. Dr Robert McLeod, Musical Director at Moray House Training College, was chosen and led the congregation and the choir from 1894 to 1898. Newhaven Parish Church was renamed Newhaven-on-Forth in 1929, and in 1974 it formed a union with Newhaven St Andrew's to form the present Newhaven Parish Church.

A welcome piece of open ground at the west end of Newhaven is provided by Starbank Park, laid out at the end of the nineteenth century on part of the garden ground of Starbank House. The central fountain, designed by George Simpson in 1910, was presented to the people of Newhaven by Thomas L. Devlin, J.P., of Newhaven. Early photographs show an ornamental fish at the fountain head and several Grecian urns around the peripheral stonework.

The Old Chain Pier Bar in Trinity Crescent marks the approximate location of the original Chain Pier constructed in 1821 by Captain Brown of the Royal Navy, as a private venture costing £4,000. The pier was five hundred feet long and four feet wide and was used by the steam packet companies operating to Stirling, Queensferry and other ports on the Forth. The pier was purchased in 1840 by the Alloa Steam Packet Company, but its popularity declined when bigger ships were unable to berth in the comparatively shallow water. After serving as a popular bathing resort for many years, the pier gradually fell into disrepair, and then suddenly into the sea during a violent storm on 18th October 1898. The Chain Pier was intended to form part of a much more ambitious scheme to provide passenger and freight travel from the centre of Edinburgh to most towns and villages along the Firth of Forth. In 1846 the journey began at Canal Street Station, which stood on the site of the present Waverley Shopping Centre at the east end of Princes Street. Canal Street was so named in anticipation of a much bigger civic plan to extend the Union Canal from Port Hopetoun in Lothian Road, round the north side of the Castle rock, to Greenside. From Canal Street Station the Edinburgh, Leith and Newhaven Railway Company cut the Scotland Street Tunnel to the north, giving

direct access by rail from the city centre to Trinity Station perched on
the hill above the Chain Pier. The line was later extended to Granton,
but the original Trinity Station building still stands north-west of York
Road, where the cutting is supported by massive buttressed masonry.

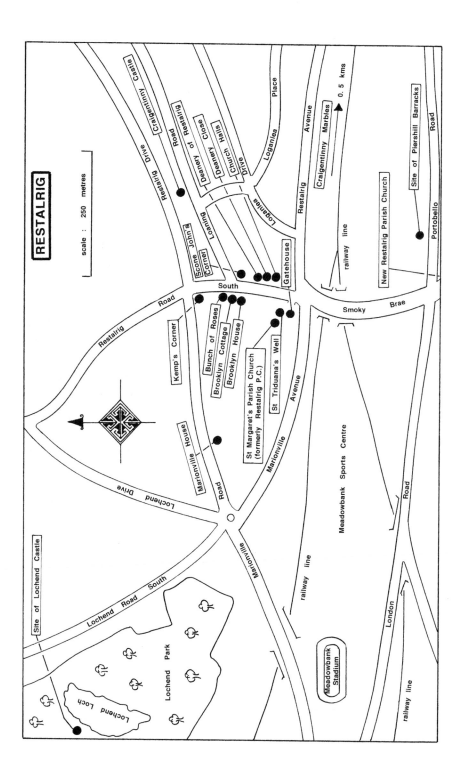

CHAPTER SEVEN

Restalrig

The old village of Restalrig lies at the foot of Smoky Brae (Restalrig Road South) a few hundred yards north of the main road and railway line from Edinburgh to London. Before the railway was built in the 1840s Restalrig was reached via Clockmill Lane which ran in a north-easterly direction from Abbeyhill, past the original site of St Margaret's Well. The Lane survived the coming of the railway but much of it was removed in 1968 when Meadowbank Sports Centre was built.

The story of Restalrig will for ever be associated with its patron saint, St Triduana. According to legend, Triduana came to Scotland in the company of St Rule and settled as a recluse at Rescobie in Angus. Her life of prayer and seclusion was not, however, sufficient protection from the amorous advances of Nectan, King of the Picts. Declaring himself mesmerised by the beauty of her eyes, he implored her to abandon her life of pious dedication and come to him. Instead, she fled to Athole 'at a place called Dunsallad' only to find that Nectan had sent word begging her to return. On learning from the King's ambassadors the reason for his great passion, Triduana plucked out her eyes, skewered them on a thorn, and handed them to the reluctant postilions for presentation to the King. With Nectan suitably discouraged, Triduana was free to lead her life as she had intended. She came to Lestalryk (Restalrig) where she spent her days healing and comforting the blind who journeyed from all parts of the country 'to mend their ene' in the special waters at Restalrig.

Not much of the original village of Restalrig survives, but what it lacks in stone and mortar is more than made up for in historical interest. There are also a few outlying places of interest well worth the few minutes it takes to reach them. The village walk is short and the terrain is flat.

This aerial photograph, taken in 1993, shows the old village of Restalrig about the centre of the picture, immediately below the roundabout. The road junction, generally known as Jock's Lodge, is at the top left-hand corner. The velodrome, part of Edinburgh City Council's Meadowbank Sports Centre, can be seen within the angle formed by the two railway lines.

Crown Copyright: Royal Commission on the Ancient and Historical Monuments of Scotland.

THE VILLAGE WALK

It is appropriate that our walk should begin at St Margaret's Parish Church, and St Triduana's Well. As we enter the old village street from the south end, the church lies on the left with the statue of St Triduana clearly visible on the roof of the adjacent chapel or well.

St Margaret's Parish Church (formerly Restalrig Parish Church) has an ancient history extending from the twelfth century to the present day, reaching its height in the fifteenth century before being eclipsed and utterly cast down at the time of the Reformation in 1560. The building of a new church in the Norman style of architecture was started in 1165 by Edward de Lestalric and completed in 1210 by Sir Thomas de Lestalric. In 1435 patronage of the church was transferred from the Bishop of St Andrews to Thomas Logan of Restalrig, whose family held the Barony of Restalrig until 1609. The church was made collegiate by James III in 1487, and received continuous support from James IV, who ordained that it should have eight prebendaries in addition to the Dean. After James IV fell at Flodden in 1513, the foundation was completed by James V but all that changed at the Reformation in 1560. Restalrig was singled out for especially zealous treatment by the reformers, who were sent to ensure 'that the Kirk of Restalrig as a monument of idolatrie be raysit and utterly casten doun and destroyed'. The Parish was transferred to South Leith Church and the church building lay desolate until around 1828, when a decision was taken to restore it. Plans were drawn up by the architect, William Burn, and Restalrig was re-opened for worship on 20th August 1837. In 1868 the Restalrig Friendly Society (who had earlier brought a successful action for ownership in the Court of Session in 1828) relinquished all rights in the church, and in 1912 it was re-established as the Parish Church of Restalrig. In April 1992 Restalrig was renamed St Margaret's as a result of a union with Lochend Church, following a period of linkage. One of the consequences of the union has been the opening of the Simpson Centre on the site of the former Lochend Church in Restalrig Road South. From the Centre, St Margaret's offers drop-in facilities and an Information Centre, where all members of the local community are made welcome.

St Margaret's Church is a rather plain rectangle with a central bellcote above the entrance doorway. Internally there are some attractive

New Restalrig Church, at Jock's Lodge, was designed by Sydney Mitchell and opened in 1902. To the left of the traffic lights are Piershill Square East and West, built on the site of the former Piershill Barracks.
Photograph by Jenni Wood.

The history of St Margaret's Church (formerly Restalrig Parish Church) can be traced back to the twelfth century. To the right of the church is St Triduana's Well, first erected by Sir Robert Logan *c.* 1438.
Photograph by Jenni Wood.

stained-glass windows: to Margaret Henderson in 1953; to Jane Morris Gibson Milligan Shaw in 1966; the Logan memorial window in 1984; and in 1980, a memorial to his wife Mabel, from George Ferguson, a former organist at the church. This latter window depicts the work of Sax Shaw.

If stones could speak, the old graveyard around St Margaret's would surely have an interesting story to tell. Although the church buildings were destroyed in 1560, the graveyard continued to be used by the Restalrig Friendly Society, and the Episcopalians in Edinburgh. During the nineteenth century several eminent figures were laid to rest at Restalrig, including Henry Brougham of Brougham Hall, distinguished politician and law reformer whose name is perpetuated in Brougham Street, near Tollcross. The family tomb of the Cauvin family is also at Restalrig, near to the church doorway. Interred there are Louis Cauvin, French Teacher in Edinburgh, who died on 22nd September 1778, and his son, also Louis Cauvin, 'for many years an eminent teacher of French in Edinburgh who bequeathed a fortune, acquired by his own skill and industry, to endow the hospital in the Parish of Duddingstone which bears his name'. He died on 19th December 1825 aged 71 years. On the east wall there is a monument to Dr Thomas Murray (1792–1872), author of the *Literary History of Galloway and Biographical Annals of the Parish of Colinton*. Some years ago Miss A. S. Cowper of Edinburgh made a special study of the graveyard, with particular reference to infant mortality. The children included many from the families of soldiers stationed at Piershill Barracks which stood to the south of Restalrig village from 1793 to 1934. Of 405 child deaths from the barracks, recorded between 1800 and 1854, fourteen were stillborn, and 276 died within the first two years of life, from such complaints as consumption, fever and water on the brain.

St Triduana's Well is easily located to the right of the main entrance to the church, its conical roof surmounted by a small statue of St Triduana. The well is believed to have been erected by Sir Robert Logan around 1438 when the family owned the Barony of Restalrig. Originally it had two storeys ; the upper storey was a chapel, whilst the lower vaulted area contained the well at which pilgrims bathed their eyes. After suffering considerable damage at the Reformation, the lower area was used as a burial chamber, principally for the Logan family. For reasons which are now obscure, the lower chamber was

This headstone in the old kirkyard at Restalrig, depicting the mitre and crook, commemorates the Right Rev. Michael Russell who became Bishop of Glasgow and Galloway in 1837: 'His body resteth here until the coming of the Lord'. *Photograph by Jenni Wood.*

covered with an earthen mound until the beginnning of the twentieth century. In 1907, under the direction of the Earl of Moray, plans were put in hand to renovate the ancient building. The earthen mound was removed to reveal the hexagonal lower chamber which was in a rather unpleasant condition from a combination of damp and the decomposition of human remains. Several stones were found which proved beyond doubt that there had been a chapel built over the well, but unfortunately too many stones were missing for an accurate restoration to be done of the upper storey. The well was located in a most interesting vaulted chamber about thirty feet across, with a centre pillar supporting a groined stone roof. The well still produces water which is kept at a fixed level by an electric pump concealed below the heavy slabs of the perimeter seat.

From time to time there has been confusion between St Triduana's Well and St Margaret's Well nearby. St Margaret's Well was originally sited on the old road from Abbeyhill, known as Clockmill Lane, but its pleasant rural setting was completely spoiled in 1850 when the North British Railway Company built extensive workshops on their adjacent land. Following a report by the antiquary, David Laing, the well was moved, stone by stone, in 1855, to an existing spring known as St David's in Holyrood Park. Today it can be seen east of Holyrood Palace, tucked into a grassy bank and giving little indication that it has ever been anywhere else. It has a small round pillar rising out of the centre of the cistern, supporting a circle of ribbed vaultwork with ornamental bosses. It is listed and illustrated in Billings' *Baronial and Ecclesiastical Antiquities of Scotland* (1852) under the heading 'St Margaret's Well, Restalrig'.

As we leave St Margaret's by the churchyard gates, turn left into the old village street at the two-storey stone and slated building. This is the old schoolhouse, dating from 1771, built by the Restalrig Friendly Society who secured a charter from 'the Ministers, Elders and Deacons of the Kirk Session of South Leith'. On the opposite side of the road the building used as the church hall has obviously had a domestic use in the past. It appears in many of the old prints as a row of two-storey houses with outside stairways, but the lower windows have been built up and the upper storey now has crowstepped stonework added over the windows. Beyond the shop fronts, on the right, the picturesque building with the projecting crowstepped gable is probably the oldest house in the village, with a date 1678 over the lintel. Immediately beside this building new iron gates lead through an open pend to Deanery Close. This development by Viewpoint Housing Association is built on the site of an old dairy. Although the byres were demolished some time ago, the house, known as Dunira, which was used in conjunction with the dairy, still stands. The significance of the name Dunira at Restalrig has never been established, nor has the identity of its former ghost. At one time the house was used by an old Edinburgh church, and became known as a place where the occasional travelling person could obtain hospitality. Whether a lost soul came back seeking refuge at Dunira is a matter of conjecture but the present owners have never been aware of any ghostly presence in the house.

Opposite Dunira a close look at the high wall shows the original entrance to the churchyard now blocked up and lacking the embellishments intended for the left-hand stone pillar. Plans, drawn up by one of the congregation in 1908 showing how the entrance could have been opened up again, were never implemented. It is here that the jougs collar hung, similar to that at Duddingston, but it was stolen many years ago and has not been replaced.

Immediately north of Dunira the old walls and gateway to the Deanery of Restalrig now give access to trade premises. Although badly worn, the gate pillars on each side are visible with the tops set out on corbels, and there are traces of an old door and window now filled in. To the north of the old Deanery is the site of the legendary Habb's Castle. One of the few references to it is by John Russell in *The Story of Leith*, in which he suggests that the name may be a corruption of Abbot's Castle. The south corner of Restalrig Road South and Loaning Road has been developed in recent years [by George Wimpey & Co.] into flats built in bronze-coloured brick. There is an interesting feature on the corner incorporating the gate of the house, St Margaret's, which stood on the site until 1982. At one time the outbuildings around St Margaret's were used as a dairy by John Wood, and later by J.M. & M. Henderson Ltd., the makers of world-famous Capital Oatcakes 'As Grannie Baked Them'. The nickname, Scone John's Corner, a fitting tribute to the Henderson family, is no longer used, nor even recalled.

At this point we turn right into Loaning Road. A few hundred yards ahead on the left is the ancient and picturesque Craigentinny House. It has been used as a Community Centre since the 1940s but its history

The sixteenth-century Craigentinny House, in Loaning Road, has been used as a
Community Centre since the 1940s. The original house, which belonged to the
Nisbets of Dean, was greatly altered in 1849 by the architect, David Rhind.
Photograph by Jenni Wood.

goes back to the end of the sixteenth century. The original house,
belonging to the Nisbets of Dean, was skilfully altered in 1849 by the
architect David Rhind in such a way that it is now difficult to distin-
guish the original house from the later additions. There is an armorial
shield over the south-facing entrance, but unfortunately it is so weath-
ered as to be indecipherable. In the middle of the eighteenth century the
house and a large part of the estate were owned by the Miller family,
discussed in more detail later in this chapter in connection with the
Craigentinny Marbles.

In the meantime, retracing our steps on Loaning Road brings us back
to the remaining short section of the old village street. Opposite the
mouth of Loaning Road is an unusual property, Brooklyn House. It has

The history of Brooklyn House in Restalrig Road South remains an enigma. The date of the original house is unknown but the impressive portico over the front door, and the tall castellated tower to the rear, were added in 1879. *Photograph by Jenni Wood.*

an impressive portico over the front door, a tall castellated tower to the rear, and a date 1879. The old maps of Edinburgh, however, show the property at least as early as 1860, with the plan of the house showing neither the portico, nor the tower. It has always been suggested that the house was owned by a gentleman who made his fortune in America and retired to Restalrig. If this was around 1879, as suggested by the date on the house, then it is possible that the owner, James Buchanan, was responsible for adding the refinements to the house on his return from America. On the other side of the lane, the small house with the shutters was called Brooklyn Cottage and must have been associated with Brooklyn House along with the stables and outbuildings to the rear. However, Brooklyn Cottage has had a separate existence for many years, being owned by the old Restalrig family of Dods when it was the Old Inn. The Dods family later moved the licensed premises into the tenement building next door where the business still flourishes. The choice of name, 'The Bunch of Roses', originates from the days when many of its clientèle were employed at St Margaret's Railway Works, to the south of the village. Occasionally the men would take the opportunity of a light refreshment when, strictly speaking, they should have been working. Unknown to them, of course, the same characteristic was frequently shared by the bosses, which meant that there was a very real risk of entering the pub during working hours and coming face to face with the gaffer. The publican, never wanting in diplomacy, placed a bunch of roses in the pub window to warn the men when it was not safe to enter.

The short village walk ends at Kemp's Corner at the junction of Restalrig Road South and Marionville Road. Kemp's Corner is not listed in the city's street directories, nor is it shown on any old map of Edinburgh, but to the older residents of Restalrig it has long been associated with the licensed grocer, Charles Arthur Kemp Snr. He came from Orkney in 1906 and established the business in Restalrig on 21st December 1908. The business was continued by his son, also Charles Arthur Kemp, until he retired in 1982.

THE EXTENDED WALK

Beyond the immediate confines of the old village, Restalrig can pride itself on having several historical buildings. Others have been

The choice of name 'The Bunch of Roses' originates from the days when the proprietor placed a bunch of roses in the window to warn the local railwaymen not to enter the pub during working hours – because the bosses were already there!
Photograph by Jenni Wood.

Kemp's Corner, showing Charles Arthur Kemp Snr. and his staff outside the shop in Restalrig Road South *c.*1935.
Courtesy of Charles Arthur Kemp Jnr.

demolished over the years, notably Hawkhill House in Lochend Road, and Restalrig House which was approached from a driveway on the corner of Restalrig Drive and Restalrig Road South. Of those remaining, the most interesting are Marionville House, the Craigentinny Marbles and the last remnants of Lochend Castle.

MARIONVILLE HOUSE

Marionville House, on the south side of Marionville Road, was built in the middle of the eighteenth century for two spinster ladies, the Misses Ramsay, who amassed a reasonable fortune from their business as milliners near Old Lyon Court in the High Street. They nicknamed their house Lappet Ha', a name which might well have gone down in history but for the much more compelling story of Captain Macrae, who lived at Marionville House with his wife around 1790. He had been retired for some years from the Irish Carabiniers and was considered to be of a generous and friendly disposition. On the debit side he had an overdeveloped sense of the respect due to a gentleman, and a fiery temper, which on more than one occasion had put him on a diet of humble pie. One such occasion was during a visit to Drumsheugh House when he threw a messenger of the law over the bannister for (rightly) serving a summons for debt on one of the guests.

During their ownership of Marionville the Macraes often arranged private theatrical performances for the entertainment of their guests, which occasionally included Sir George Ramsay of Banff and Lady Ramsay. At the end of a production one evening at the Old Theatre Royal, Macrae was escorting a lady from the theatre and arranging transport to take her home. He ordered a 'chair' and was about to help the lady into it when a footman stepped forward and claimed that he had already ordered the chair for his employer. In fact the footman was so drunk that he had forgotten that his employer had gone home earlier in the evening. Macrae, in his characteristic manner, took up the challenge, struck the footman several times and created a fracas in which the guests and onlookers were inclined to take sides. When Macrae discovered the next day that the drunken footman was in the employment of Lady Ramsay, he went to her house and apologised. Unfortunately, the footman, James Merry, had already decided to have his revenge and had issued a writ for damages against the Captain.

Captain Macrae of Marionville House, the fiery-tempered duellist, with the inset
showing him at target practice.
From Kay's Original Portraits.

This incensed Macrae so much that he wrote to Sir George Ramsay demanding either that the writ be withdrawn or, alternatively, that James Merry be dismissed from his post. To Macrae's astonishment Sir George wrote back to say that he could not intervene. The ensuing correspondence grew more and more acrimonious until the two gentlemen, hellbent on proving that they were each men of honour, met at 12 noon at Ward's Inn near Musselburgh Links – complete with guns, seconds, and Benjamin Bell the surgeon. Captain Macrae expressed the wish that the matter be settled amicably. There were proposals and counter-proposals but no agreement was reached. The parties proceeded to the Links and measured off twelve paces. On the signal being given, Sir George fired first, the bullet passing through the collar of Macrae's coat and slightly grazing his neck. At that, Captain Macrae, who had always maintained that he would fire in the air, took deliberate aim and brought Sir George to the ground with a shot from which he did not recover. Public feeling ran high against Macrae, who was accused of having had extensive pistol practice before the duel. He fled to France. A summons was issued for his arrest but he did not appear, and sentence of outlawry was passed. He died in obscurity on 16th January 1820, the victim of his own fiery temper.

CRAIGENTINNY MARBLES

In Craigentinny Crescent another story lies buried, closely linked to Craigentinny House which we visited in Loaning Road. In the middle of the eighteenth century the house and a large part of the estate were bought by William Miller, a prosperous seed merchant in Edinburgh. Later the property passed to his son, also named William. Fairly late in life the younger William Miller married Miss Rawson, the couple living in London and Paris, and producing a son, William Henry Miller, born in 1789. He spent most of his life in England; he never married and was something of a recluse by nature; but he became Member of Parliament for Newcastle-under-Lyme in 1830. In the latter part of his life he developed a great interest in collecting books for his library at his Buckinghamshire home, Britwell Court. He earned himself the nickname 'Measure Miller' from his eccentric habit of visiting various book sales and measuring precisely the size of each volume before deciding if it would enhance his existing collection. When he died in Edinburgh

This huge mausoleum, the Craigentinny Marbles, now towering above the bungalows in Craigentinny Crescent, was erected to the memory of William Henry Miller (1789–1848) and his family.
Photograph by Jenni Wood.

in 1848 he bequeathed his library, 'containing for rarity and condition an unrivalled collection of books', to his old college at Cambridge, but the conditions attached to the gift were so complicated that the bequest was not taken up. By then the public were perhaps beginning to get some idea of just how eccentric Miller had been. In the words of Daniel Wilson, the Edinburgh historian, Miller 'was notable for his spare figure, thin treble voice and total absence of beard', characteristics which led the villagers of Restalrig to assert that he was either a woman or 'a fairy changeling'. Whatever he was, he took his secret to the grave and made sure that it would not be lightly uncovered. Some six weeks after his death, the funeral cortège left Craigentinny House for a remote spot on his own estate where, it is said, he was interred at a depth of forty feet below the curious onlookers. A squad of workmen laboured long and hard to fill the grave, which was later capped by a huge mausoleum-type structure, now known locally as the Craigentinny Marbles. The tomb stands high above the bungalows in Craigentinny Crescent, but it has kept its secret well:

THIS MONUMENT WAS ERECTED TO THE MEMORY OF
WILLIAM HENRY MILLER
AND HIS PARENTS
WILLIAM MILLER AND MARTHA RAWSON OR MILLER

HERE ARE INTERRED
MARTHA MILLER
DIED 11TH JANUARY 1827
WILLIAM HENRY MILLER
M.P. FOR NEWCASTLE-UNDER-LYME
BORN 13TH FEBRUARY 1789 DIED 31ST OCTOBER 1848
SARAH MARSH
BORN 20TH APRIL 1792 DIED 6TH AUGUST 1860
ELLEN MARSH
BORN 29TH AUGUST 1801 DIED 4TH NOVEMBER 1861

ALL OF CRAIGENTINNY AND BRITWELL
BUCKINGHAMSHIRE
THE SITE WAS CONSECRATED ON 13TH SEPTEMBER 1860
THE SCULPTURES WERE ADDED IN 1866

ARCHITECT   SCULPTOR
DAVID RHIND   ALFRED GATLEY
EDINBURGH   ROME

Gatley's work, carved in low relief, depicts 'The Overthrow of Pharaoh in the Red Sea' and 'The Song of Moses and Miriam'.

LOCHEND CASTLE

On the west side of Lochend Road South, part of the old estate of the Logans is now laid out as a public park around what remains of

Lochend Loch. Near the north entrance a sixteenth-century dovecot stands on ground once known as Logan Lea. The alternative name, Kilnacre, is believed to date from the mid-seventeenth century when the dovecot may have been used as a kiln for disinfection during the plague of 1645. At the south end of the park, high on the precipitous rock face, are the remnants of a very old building variously described as Lochend Castle, Lochend House or Restalrig Castle, ancestral seat of the Logans of Restalrig, whose baronetcy can be traced back to the fourteenth century. The dominance of the Logan family endured until the fifteenth century, after which there was a gradual dissipation of their wealth and influence, culminating in the disastrous Gowrie Conspiracy.

In 1600 John 3rd Earl of Gowrie and his brother Alexander, Master of Ruthven, conspired to assassinate James VI, but the plot was unsuccessful and they were overpowered and killed in Gowrie House at Perth. To reinforce the sense of public outrage and to give due weight to the seriousness of the offence their bodies were brought to Edinburgh where they were 'hanged quartered and beheaded'. Sir Robert Logan lived out his life in peace, dying in 1606. Although Sir Robert was dead and gone, the rumours were not so easily buried. In 1608 George Sprott, a notary from Eyemouth, who had worked on various transactions with Sir Robert Logan, began to talk, linking the name of Sir Robert with the Gowrie Conspiracy. Sprott was arrested, charged with concealing treason, found guilty, and hanged on 12th August 1608. Even after Sprott was hanged, his suspect evidence was examined again and again until five letters, allegedly written by Sir Robert Logan confirming his involvement in the Conspiracy, were produced in court and attested by witnesses. In 1609 Sir Robert was 'summoned' to appear before the court. His remains were exhumed, the body was laid before the court and on a finding of guilty, sentence of forfeiture was passed on his title, lands and property. The case must surely be unusual in legal history, the accused having spent many hours in the box without being able to speak a single word in his own defence! It is generally considered that Sir Robert Logan was convicted on evidence which, to say the least, was tenuous and inconclusive, but that did not prevent his estates passing to Lord Balmerino who held them until he, too, was dispossessed for being on the losing side at the time of the '45 Rebellion.

Although Lochend Castle was destroyed many years ago, the commanding site above the water is now occupied by another interesting old house used as Lochend Children's Centre. The remaining part of the castle with the distinctive stepped chimney is incorporated in the caretaker's house to the west of the main building.

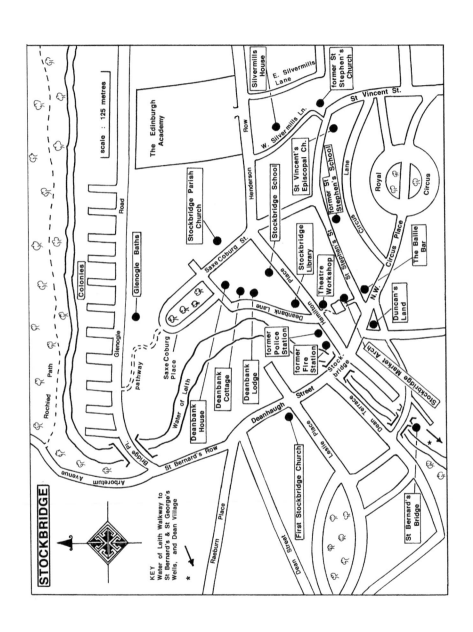

CHAPTER 8

Stockbridge

Less than a mile north of Princes Street is Stockbridge, Edinburgh's New Town village, which straddles the Water of Leith between the older communities of Dean to the west, and Canonmills to the east. Although Stockbridge cannot claim great antiquity, its two centuries of recorded history provide abundant evidence of its contribution to the history and character of Edinburgh. Its principal claim to fame is undoubtedly the long list of artists, historians, and men and women of letters, who were either born in the village, or lived there at a significant time in their careers. In the early nineteenth century its proximity to the New Town, combined with plenty of space, made it a popular area in which to establish some of the great new educational institutions of the day. Later, the Victorian era brought the Colonies, tenement buildings, Board schools and public transport in the form of cable cars.

Nowadays, Stockbridge has the bustle and confidence of a prosperous community of fashionable housing, restaurants, shops and businesses, sitting side by side with some of the earliest relics of the old village. Our walk involves some modest inclines, and the opportunity to include a short section of the Water of Leith Walkway.

The T-shaped building near the centre of the picture is The Edinburgh Academy, designed by the architect William Burn, with its front entrance facing towards Henderson Row. To the left of the Academy is the former Junior School of Donaldson's School for the Deaf which was used in the filming of *The Prime of Miss Jean Brodie* in 1968. Many of the old industrial buildings at Silvermills can be seen in the right-hand corner.

Courtesy of The Edinburgh Academy. Photograph by Ferranti Ltd., Edinburgh.

THE VILLAGE WALK

Our walk begins in the centre of the old village at the Stoke or Stock Bridge which still carries the main traffic flow across the Water of Leith. On each of the parapets there is a plaque confirming that the stone bridge was first erected in 1786 and was widened and improved in 1900–01 by the engineer, David C. Proudfoot. Prior to 1786 development of the village to the north-west of the river was seriously limited by the lack of a proper bridge: wheeled vehicles could only cross by the ford, and pedestrians used a light wooden bridge.

Near the present bridge there are two prominent landmarks which have been part of the skyline for many years. One is the clock tower of the old Edinburgh Savings Bank beside the bridge. The other, larger tower (on the corner of Leslie Place and Deanhaugh Street) is all that remains of Stockbridge Church, most of which was demolished in 1980 to make way for sheltered housing. To continue our walk we leave the

All passengers aboard the Edinburgh & District Tramways Company cable car at Comely Bank terminus, ready for the journey via Stockbridge to Princes Street, *c.* 1914.
Courtesy of D. L. G. Hunter.

The centre of Stockbridge is dominated by two spires. The one with the clock was occupied by the former Edinburgh Savings Bank (later the Trustee Savings Bank), and the one on the left is all that remains of Stockbridge Church, most of which was demolished in 1980 for the construction of sheltered housing.
Photograph by Jenni Wood.

Stock Bridge and turn east into Hamilton Place which was built on the line of a much older road linking Stockbridge to Silvermills and Canonmills. The main places of interest are probably best seen from the south pavement. Two squat buildings, with their backs to the Water of Leith, have been greatly altered internally from the days when they were used as the local fire station and police station. The one on the left (the fire station) is now a public toilet, and the one on the right (the police station) is a restaurant. Ahead, on the corner of Dean Bank Lane, is Stockbridge Library, built in red sandstone to designs by the architect H. Ramsay Taylor. Dating from 1898, it is one of several

similar libraries established with financial assistance from Thomas
Nelson, the Edinburgh printer and publisher.

Also in Hamilton Place, opposite the mouth of Dean Bank Lane, is
the former Wesley Hall now occupied by the popular arts venue
Theatre Workshop. This thriving theatre, cafe and community arts
resource moved to Stockbridge in 1975 and acts as a link between the
community and professional sectors of theatre. It places special emphasis on reaching people who have not previously benefited fully from the
arts. In addition to its own touring and in-house productions, it is
Edinburgh's main venue for small-scale national and international visiting companies.

The large triangle of ground bounded by Dean Park Lane, Saxe
Coburg Street and Hamilton Place was first developed in the late
eighteenth century, and still retains several properties of that period.
The most interesting, whose front entrance is screened from the street
by a high stone wall, is Deanbank House on the corner of the Lane and
Saxe Coburg Street. It is two storeys in height with urns at the corners,
on the front, and two single-storey wings at the back. Two adjacent

The St Stephen's Motor & Cycle Depot was run by Engel Nelson at No. 10
Hamilton Place in the 1920s.
Courtesy of I. McMurtrie.

A horse-drawn fire engine ready for action outside the Fire Station in Hamilton Place, c. 1900.
Courtesy of Lothian & Borders Fire Brigade.

properties date from the same period. The smaller one is Deanbank Cottage, and the more extensive one, with the pedimented entrance gateway, is Deanbank Lodge. Each has been greatly altered from its original setting in gardens laid out with lawns and shrubberies. Much of the development at Deanbank Lodge was completed when it was occupied by the Dean Bank Institution for the Reformation of Juvenile Female Delinquents, first established in 1832. An endless succession of young girls were referred there, many after release from the Bridewell, which was founded in 1791 in Regent Road as Edinburgh's new House of Correction. Case histories for the year 1840 suggest that, for some, confinement to Dean Bank Institution could follow from comparatively minor offences:

> Case 1 – Her fault was stealing from her mistress – she is seemingly friendless – had never attended a place of worship – two years in Dean Bank Institution.

Case 2 – Well educated but wholly ignorant of religion – had never received religious instruction – her fault was selling a book which had been stolen by her brother.

The ages of the twenty-four inmates ranged from ten to fifteen years, and all were equally subjected to the rigours of 'moral restraint, religious influence and training in branches of female industry'. A surviving, undated photograph, taken in the garden of the Institution, shows a group of about twenty-six girls, all apparently well dressed and well nourished, in the charge of four or five mature staff.

Saxe Coburg Place, with the central garden ground, was unfortunately never finished according to the architect's plans. The original design was by James Milne, in 1821, but part of the ground was later taken over by Adam O. Turnbull who went bankrupt before the street was finished. The result is a rather ugly gap at the north-west end which, if nothing else, provides us with the opportunity to see the Colonies and Glenogle Baths from an elevated position. The Colonies are two-storey buildings, plus dormers, in a series of short terraces between Glenogle Road and the Water of Leith. The basic lay-out is unusual in that the upper and lower flats (of the same building) are set back to back, i.e. the lower flat is entered from one street whilst the upper flat is reached from the adjacent street. The history and development of the Colonies is a most interesting story, ably written and illustrated by Rosemary J. Pipes in *The Colonies of Stockbridge*. The houses, constructed from 1861 by the Edinburgh Co-operative Building Company Limited, were intended to provide low-priced housing for working people to buy or rent, an aim admirably achieved from the early days of the Co-operative. Two of the terraces bear the names of supporters of self-help housing, namely Hugh Miller, stonemason, writer, journalist and geologist, and Hugh Gilzean Reid, journalist and later Liberal M.P. Several other terraces were named after principal participants in the original company: James Colville, stonemason and first manager of the Co-operative; David Bell, joiner and one-time chairman; and James Collins, stonemason and also one-time chairman.

The gap in the façade of Saxe Coburg Place was partially, but not very appropriately, filled by the construction of Glenogle Baths, designed by the City Architect, Robert Morham, and built between 1897 and 1900. There is a square tower in red sandstone on three corners but not on the corner nearest to Saxe Coburg Place, where the

Stockbridge Parish Church (previously St Bernard's Stockbridge) in Saxe Coburg Street was designed by the architect James Milne, and opened on 16th November 1823.
Photograph by Jenni Wood.

classical frontage is in ashlar, presumably in an attempt to lessen the impact on the remainder of the street. On the south-east section of Saxe Coburg Street (originally named West Claremont Street) is the former St Bernard's Church, later St Bernard's Stockbridge and now Stockbridge Parish Church from 1992. It has a distinctive classical façade by James Milne, with pairs of Ionic pillars supporting a pediment and square clock tower. The church was opened on 16th November 1823 under the name St Cuthbert's Chapel of Ease. Its first minister was the Rev. James Henderson who later became a Moderator of the General Assembly. During the time of the Rev. James MacFarlane (who later went to Duddingston) the Chapel of Ease was made a parish church in 1834, but this was suspended at the Disruption in 1843. The Rev. Alexander W. Brown had been minister for less than a year when he 'came out' with the Kirk Session and joined the historic procession from St Andrew's Church in George Street to Tanfield Hall at Canonmills on 18th May 1843 which marked the founding of the Free Church of Scotland. Perhaps the most famous minister was the Rev. George Matheson, the 'Blind Seer' who wrote many books and hymns, notably O *Love that wilt not let me go.*

Three important educational institutions were established within a few hundred yards of one another to the south of Saxe Coburg Street. In chronological order they were: the Institution for the Education of Deaf and Dumb Children in 1823 in Henderson Row; the Edinburgh Academy in 1824 also in Henderson Row; and Stockbridge Primary School in 1877 in Hamilton Place. For the purpose of our walk we shall take them in reverse order.

Stockbridge Primary School in Hamilton Place was designed in 1874 in the Gothic style by R. Rowand Anderson, as one of the earliest Board Schools established under the Education Act of 1872. It was opened, as Stockbridge Public School, on 12th January 1877 with 537 pupils, most of whom lived locally and had previously attended one of the small parochial schools attached to the various churches. Although Stockbridge was considered, architecturally, as one of the best Board Schools of that era, subsequent generations of staff and pupils have been constantly harassed by the inconvenient internal lay-out, which does not have orthodox corridors between different parts of the building. Various references in the school logs, meticulously kept since 1877, highlight periods of extreme austerity during each of the two World

Wars. Large-scale reorganisation of classes was required during the First World War when Flora Stevenson's School, at Comely Bank, was made into a military hospital, and the pupils were transferred to Stockbridge. The extra hands were, however, put to good use when the pupils donated an assortment of home comforts for the war effort: twenty pairs of socks, three knitted face cloths, two pyjama cords and a knitted bed rug. At the outbreak of the Second World War, in 1939, many parents and children were evacuated to Speyside. Post-war events included a Coronation Service held at St Bernard's Davidson Church, and a visit to the Ritz Cinema, in Rodney Street, on 12th June 1953 to see *Elizabeth is Queen*. At the present day Stockbridge Primary, in common with many Edinburgh schools, is closely involved with the community around it, and is conscious of its long history. The former Dean Bank Institution building, adjacent to the school, has been used over the years as an annexe, and in 1996 the interior of the main school building was extensively refurbished.

For many years Edinburgh has been closely involved in the education of children with speech and hearing difficulties. Indeed the district of Dumbiedykes, on the south side of the city, takes its name from a house near Holyrood Park in which Mr Braidwood, an instructor of the 'deaf and dumb', resided with his pupils. The school was operating around 1764 and is believed to have been the first of its kind in the world. Better facilities and training were provided in 1810 with the founding of the Institution for the Education of Deaf and Dumb Children in Chessel's Court in the Canongate. Although this new Institution was almost completely dependent upon charitable contributions, it was able to acquire a much more spacious site in 1823 for the erection of a new building, designed by James Gillespie Graham, in Distillery Park on the north side of Henderson Row. This specialised area of child education received another substantial impetus on the death, in 1830, of James Donaldson, publisher and printer of West Bow, who left the sum of £210,000 'to build and found an hospital for boys and girls to be called Donaldson's Hospital preferring those of the name Donaldson and Marshall to be after the plan of the Orphan Hospital in Edinburgh and John Watson's Hospital'. The result was Playfair's magnificently ornate quadrangle at West Coates, commenced in 1841 but not finished until 1851. Pupils were admitted on 16th October 1850, and for almost a century Donaldson's Hospital at West Coates and the Institution for the Education of Deaf and Dumb Children at Stockbridge maintained separate identities, albeit engaged in the same type of work. In 1938 the two schools combined to form Donaldson's School for the Deaf, although the enabling Act of Parliament was not passed until 1953. Senior pupils were taught at West Coates and junior pupils at Henderson Row. A brief but memorable event occurred at the Henderson Row site on 20th July 1968 when 20th Century Fox arrived to film Muriel Spark's *The Prime of Miss Jean Brodie*, starring Maggie Smith as Miss Brodie. The solid gate piers acquired additional finials, and a decorative iron over-gate temporarily converted Donaldson's School to the Marcia Blaine School for Girls. In 1977, following reorganisation of Donaldson's at West Coates, the Henderson Row building was sold to its worthy neighbour, the Edinburgh Academy. In 1992 Donaldson's School was renamed Donaldson's College to reflect more accurately the range of people with whom it works.

Edinburgh Academy, perhaps more so than any other school in Edinburgh, was forged on the anvil of discontent with the educational philosophy of the day. In Edinburgh, at the beginning of the nineteenth century, classical education was mainly in the hands of the Town Council's own High School, but several factors were operating in favour of a new classical school in the New Town. The founders of the Edinburgh Academy were concerned that the High School was not providing the type of education which Scotland needed to compete with England for the top positions in running the Empire. Scotland was good at producing doctors and advocates but it also needed to be able to compete with the English Public Schools for places at Oxford and Cambridge. The idea of a new classical school in the city was enthusiastically taken up and brought to fruition by two leading Whigs of the day (both of whom had been educated at the High School), namely Henry Cockburn (later Lord Cockburn) and Leonard Horner. When they shrewdly crossed the political divide by asking John Russel W. S. to complete the triumvirate, and so make the project acceptable to the influential high Tory, Sir Walter Scott, success appeared to be within their grasp. Despite considerable opposition from some members of Edinburgh Town Council steady progress was made. The site in Henderson Row, previously proposed by Cockburn and Horner, was acquired, and William Burn, the architect, was asked to modify his earlier drawings to bring costs within the modest budget of £13,000.

The Hailes game (described in *The Clacken and the Slate* as a cross between the Eton Wall Game and shinty) in full swing on the Front Yards of The Edinburgh Academy. The hollow rubber ball is struck with a clacken which resembles a large wooden spoon. The Greek inscription above the pillars is the school motto: *Education is the mother of both Wisdom and Virtue.*
Courtesy of The Edinburgh Academy.

The first Rector was appointed – Dr John Williams, formerly of Winchester and of Lampeter College in Wales – and the school was opened on 1st October 1824. The new Edinburgh Academy adopted a system of instruction based generally on the High School system but with more emphasis on Greek, English, Geography and Arithmetic. The Rector, perhaps hopeful that he was writing the first page of a long history, requested one boon from an enlightened public – that they would not be hasty in their censure, nor premature in their applause. A century and a half later, after the Academy had produced a long line

R. C. Howells, organist and choir master at The Edinburgh Academy, conducting the string orchestra in the Oval Hall in the mid-1950s.
Courtesy of The Edinburgh Academy.

of distinguished leaders in every walk of life, Magnus Magnusson, in
The Clacken and the Slate, told the fascinating story of the Edinburgh
Academy from 1824 to 1974 'in its context of time and place, in
Edinburgh, in Scotland, in the development of education'.

Silvermills lies in the dip between Henderson Row and the east section of St Stephen Street. Apparently it takes its name from the time
when ore from a small silver mine at Linlithgow was brought to the village for refining. The name dates from at least the sixteenth century,
preceding Stockbridge by more then a century. Over the years the district has had a strong industrial presence, linked, no doubt, to the
existence of the lade which provided water power from the Water of
Leith. After a long period of neglect in recent years, Silvermills has
again attracted new development, and the renovation of some of the
older properties. The jewel in the crown is undoubtedly Silvermills
House (in West Silvermills Lane) dating from 1760, in which the artist
brothers, Robert Scott Lauder, R.S.A. (1803–69) and James Eckford
Lauder, R.S.A. (1811–69), were born.

Looking south from Silvermills it is possible to appreciate at least
some of the problems which beset William H. Playfair in his design for
the former burgh church of St Stephen's at the east end of St Stephen
Street. It is probably the most significant landmark in the district, built
between 1827 and 1828. The site was difficult to develop, the natural
contours of the ground falling away steeply to the north, yet present-
ing an uninterrupted vista southwards and uphill to George Street.
These factors undoubtedly influenced Playfair in his final design, which
is basically a square, diagonally sited, with the north and south corners
cut off. The natural ground levels dictated that the imposing south
doorway, at the head of a huge flight of steps, entered the church at
gallery level, while entry to the main body of the church was by two
comparatively modest side doors. At first sight, the main entrance
appears to face exactly southwards to the statue of William Pitt at the
junction of Frederick Street and George Street, but, in fact, the whole
church is set slightly askew to the west. That does not, however,
detract significantly from the boldness of the design or from the
majesty of its great tower 162 feet in height. Though generally considered to have met most of the challenges of this awkward site, the
absence of lateral support on each side of the yawning entrance
prompted Professor Blackie to voice the opinion that it was like 'a

The massive tower of the former St Stephen's Church by William H. Playfair, built 1827–1828, with the much smaller St Vincent's Episcopal Church, 1857, on the left.
Photograph by the late A. C. Robson.

mouth without cheeks'. Internally there were also problems with the acoustics, at least one preacher taking the view that addressing his flock was more like shouting for a lost sheep in a quarry! This latter problem was cured in the mid-1950s when extensive reorganisation of the interior was undertaken by the architect Gilbert H. Jenkins of London. A reinforced concrete floor was put in at gallery level to create the main body of the new church, leaving the lower area for hall accommodation and a small theatre. After being used continuously for public worship from 1828, St Stephen's Church was closed in 1992, when the congregation united with St Bernard's Stockbridge in Saxe Coburg Street to form Stockbridge Parish Church. The former St Stephen's Church building is now occupied as St Stephen's Centre which includes the Playfair Cafe. The Sonrise Christian Fellowship meet each Sunday, and numerous organisations use the halls during the week, including Mother and Toddler Groups, Tai Chi Classes (Chinese meditation), the Stockbridge Pipe Band, the Stockbridge Community Orchestra and various Self-Help Groups.

St Vincent's Episcopal Church was built on the opposite corner to St Stephen's, in 1857, to designs by J. W. H. and J. M. Hay of Liverpool. The north aisle, entrance porch and shortened spire face towards St Stephen Street while the chancel gable faces St Vincent Street. Internally there are several stained-glass windows depicting heraldic subjects in keeping with the heraldic shields on the gallery balustrade and the ceiling. The church was purchased in 1874 by William Forbes Skene W. S., who gifted it to the Scottish Episcopal Church in memory of his parents, James Skene of Rubislaw and Jane Forbes. By 1961, however, the congregation had diminished to such an extent that St Vincent's became a Mission under St Paul and St George's in York Place. On St Lazarus' Day, 17th December, 1967 St Vincent's was inaugurated as a Chapel of the Commandery of Lochore in the Military and Hospitaller Order of St Lazarus of Jerusalem, but that connection no longer exists.

At this point in our walk we turn back towards the centre of Stockbridge. The section of St Stephen Street between West Silvermills Lane and Clarence Street was occupied by Cinderellas Rockerfellas until it was burned down in 1993. This cacophonous 'mecca' for the young at heart had a variety of uses in former years, including a skating rink, music hall, theatre, riding academy and cinema. Further along St Stephen Street, on the left-hand side, are the former St Stephen's Church Halls, the former St Vincent's Church Hall, and St Stephen's School dating from 1835, now in commercial use. High on the front of the former school building is an open Bible, carved in stone, with the

Fire fighting, with the standard equipment of the day, at Tod's Flour Mill in
Baker's Place on 16th July 1901.
Courtesy of Lothian & Borders Fire Brigade.

inscription THOSE THAT SEEK ME EARLY SHALL FIND ME. At St
Stephen Place the ornate entrance archway is all that remains of
Stockbridge Market, designed in 1824 by Archibald Scott to include
stalls for fish, poultry, fruit and vegetables. There is a right of way
through the archway which takes us back to the Stock Bridge, or alternatively we can continue our walk to visit the places of interest to the
west of the bridge.

The extended walk begins, but hopefully does not end, at the Bailie
Bar on the south-east corner of St Stephen Street and North West Circus
Place. Cross North West Circus Place into Gloucester Street, previously
part of Kirk Loan or Church Street which ran from St Cuthbert's Parish
Church at the West End to Stockbridge. At the corner of Gloucester
Street and India Place is Duncan's Land, now a restaurant, in which the

Duncan's Land (now occupied as a restaurant) in Gloucester Street in which the artist David Roberts was born in 1796. The lintel stone, with the date 1605, was brought from a house in the Lawnmarket which was demolished to make way for Bank Street at the top of the Mound.
Photograph by Jenni Wood.

artist David Roberts was born in 1796. The house is believed to have been built of stones taken from houses in the Lawnmarket demolished to allow the opening up of Bank Street at the top of the Mound. Across the lintel stone of Duncan's Land, which also came from the Lawnmarket, is the inscription: FEAR GOD ONLYE 1605 IR.

Many years ago, the area between Leslie Place and Dean Terrace was occupied by two of the district's principal houses, Deanhaugh House and St Bernard's House. Whilst nothing remains of them now, their historical associations are sufficiently strong to justify their inclusion.

Deanhaugh House, of uncertain date, survived until 1880 when it was swept away in the construction of the buildings on the south side of Leslie Place. The house was owned by James Leslie whose widow, Ann Leslie, married Henry Raeburn the celebrated portrait painter. Raeburn was born on 4th March 1756 in a modest cottage to the west of what is now Kerr Street, the younger son of William Raeburn, a yarn-boiler at Stockbridge. After visiting London and Rome, Henry Raeburn returned to Edinburgh, setting up a studio in George Street in 1787 and moving to York Place in 1798. He became Scotland's foremost portrait painter and was knighted at a ceremony at Hopetoun House during George IV's visit to Edinburgh in 1822. He died on 8th July 1823 at the age of sixty-seven. Whilst at Stockbridge, Raeburn was resident at Deanhaugh House and also at the much grander St Bernard's House, to the south-west: both were a far cry from the modest house in which he was born.

St Bernard's House, the principal mansion of old Stockbridge, had earned itself a place in history even before the arrival of Henry Raeburn. Prior to Raeburn's occupation, St Bernard's was owned by the humorous and eccentric Walter Ross, Writer to the Signet and Registrar of Distillery Licences in Scotland. He was a great collector of antiquities and spent much of his time pursuing his absorbing hobby of ornamental gardening. The story is told of how he dealt with unwelcome intruders on his estate after the hours of darkness. He let it be known in the village that his grounds were protected by an array of spring-guns and mantraps, but unfortunately no one believed him, and the vandalism continued. In a last attempt to convince the villagers that he was not just *pulling* their leg, old Ross drew upon his macabre sense of humour. He acquired a human leg from the Royal Infirmary, dressed it up in a stocking, shoe and buckle and sent it round the village with the town crier, who held it aloft, proclaiming that it had been found the previous night on Mr Ross's estate, and offering to restore it to anyone who could make up the matching pair. With the intruders suitably discouraged, Ross returned to improving his estate. His crowning achievement was undoubtedly his own Folly, erected on the highest point of ground in the south-west corner of the estate. It was about forty feet high, by about twenty feet square, consisting of two rooms one above the other, the upper floor being reached by an outside stairway which wound round three sides of the tower. From a distance it gave the impression of an old rusticated Border peel or tower-house. When he died suddenly and mysteriously on 11th March 1789 his body, at his own request, was kept eight days and then interred in the under part of the tower with the top of his coffin left open. Several years later, in 1818, when the surrounding area was being redeveloped, he was re-interred in St Cuthbert's Churchyard, and Ross's Folly was eventually demolished in 1825.

St Bernard's Bridge carries India Place across the Water of Leith. The bridge was constructed in 1824 but the flight of steps down to the Water of Leith Walkway was not added until 1887.
Photograph by Jenni Wood.

The upper section of St Bernard's Well is a domed temple of ten plain Doric columns, within which stands a statue of Hygeia.
Photograph by Jenni Wood.

To visit St Bernard's Well and the smaller St George's Well go west-wards on Saunders Street and walk under the arched and buttressed St Bernard's Bridge, built in 1824 to carry India Place across the Water of Leith. A few hundred yards along the Water of Leith Walkway is St Bernard's Well on the south bank. Lord Gardenstone, a Senator of the College of Justice, believing that he had benefited from the medicinal properties of the water, commissioned Alexander Nasmyth, in 1788, to build the present well on the site of a much smaller structure. The base is constructed of very large, roughly hewn stones, supporting a circular, domed temple of ten plain Doric columns, within which stands a statue of Hygeia. The statue is not the original, having been replaced in 1887 when the well was restored at the expense of William Nelson.

St Bernard's Well on the banks of the Water of Leith was commissioned in 1788 by Lord Gardenstone, Senator of the College of Justice, who believed that he had benefited from the medicinal properties of the spring water.
Photograph by Jenni Wood.

Beside the well, on its east side, a stone tablet encircles a low relief medallion of William Nelson by the sculptor John Rhind. Above it are the words THE LIBERAL DEVISETH LIBERAL THINGS, and the entwined initials W. N.

A few hundred yards upstream from St Bernard's Well is the much less impressive St George's Well built high above the water's edge, with a pedimented gable containing the date 1810 at the front, a single chimney on the west side, and a round-nosed gable end to the rear. At this point on the Walkway we are within a few minutes' walk of the Dean Bridge and the Dean Village which we visited in Chapter 4. Alternatively, we can retrace our steps by St Bernard's Bridge and Saunders Street, back to the Stock Bridge. In addition to its historical associations Stockbridge has many excellent shops, restaurants and hostelries well worth a visit.

Suggestions for Further Reading

GENERAL

Author	Title	Year of Publication
Birrell, J.F.	*An Edinburgh Alphabet*	1980
—	*Book of the Old Edinburgh Club*	1908 to date
Geddie, John	*The Fringes of Edinburgh*	1926
Gifford, John, McWilliam, Colin Walker, David	*The Buildings of Scotland: Edinburgh*	1984
Grant, James	*Old and New Edinburgh*	1882
Gray, W. Forbes	*Historic Churches of Edinburgh*	1940
Harris, Stuart	*The Place Names of Edinburgh*	1996
McKean, Charles	*Edinburgh: An Illustrated Architectural Guide*	1992
McArthur, Margaret	*Bonnie Blackhall*	1995
Mullay, Sandy	*The Edinburgh Encyclopaedia*	1996
Nimmo, Ian	*Edinburgh's Green Heritage*	1996
Royal Commission on the Ancient and Historical Monuments of Scotland	*The City of Edinburgh*	1951
Thomas, Brendan	*The Last Picture Shows: Edinburgh*	1984

CORSTORPHINE

Beveridge, A.	*Some Corstorphine Street Names*	1983
Corstorphine Trust	*Corstorphine Notes*	1975
Cowper, A.S.	*Historic Corstorphine and Roundabout* 4 volumes	1992
Dey, William G.	*St Ann's, Corstorphine*	1966
Milligan, Oswald B.	*Corstorphine and its Parish Church*	1929
Scottish Arts Council	*Dovecot Tapestries Jubilee Exhibition 1912–1962*	1962
Scottish Arts Council	*Small Tapestries*	1976
Scottish Arts Council	*Master Weavers: Tapestry from the Dovecot Studios 1912–1980*	1980

| Selway, G. Upton | A Mid-Lothian Village | 1890 |
| Thomson, D. M. | The Corstorphine Heirloom | 1946 |

CRAMOND

Breeze, David J.	The Northern Frontiers of Roman Britain	1982
Cadell, Patrick	The Iron Mills at Cramond	1973
Cramond Heritage Trust	Cramond Kirkyard: Memorial Inscriptions	1993
Cramond Heritage Trust	Cramond	1996
Sidgwick, Frank (editor)	The Complete Marjory Fleming	1934
Small, John	Castles and Mansions of the Lothians	1883
Wood, John P.	The Antient and Modern State of the Parish of Cramond	1794, reprinted 1994

DAVIDSON'S MAINS

Fairley, John A.	Lauriston Castle	1925
Philip, Rev. Adam	The Ancestry of Randall Thomas Davidson D.D., Archbishop of Canterbury	1903
Rowan, Martha	Lauriston Castle	1974
Taylor, James	Lord Jeffrey and Craigcrook	1892

DEAN

Ballantine, James	The Miller of Deanhaugh	1844
Coghill, Hamish	Dicovering the Water of Leith	1988
Environmental Resource Centre	The Water of Leith Trail: Dean to Stockbridge	1982
Geddie, John	The Home Country of R. L. Stevenson	1898
Hill, Cumberland	Historic Memorials & Reminiscences of Stockbridge and the Water of Leith	1887
Jamieson, Stanley (editor)	The Water of Leith	1984
Skinner, Basil	The House on the Bridge	1982

DUDDINGSTON

Baird, William	Annals of Duddingston and Portobello	1898
Chambers, Robert	The Innocent Railway	1847
Cruikshank, W. G.	Duddingston Kirk and Village	1979
Napier, Robert W.	John Thomson of Duddingston	1919
Smith, David B.	Curling: an Illustrated History	1981
Speedy, Tom	Craigmillar and its Environs	1892
Warrender, Margaret	Walks near Edinburgh	1895

NEWHAVEN

Anderson, James	*Report on ship canal from Newhaven to Leith*	1834
Burnett, Rev. A. Ian	*The Church of Newhaven-on-Forth*	1936
Campbell, Alex.	*The History of Leith*	1827
Cupples, Mrs George	*Newhaven: Its Origin and History*	1888
McGowran, Tom	*Newhaven on Forth*	1985
Wallace, Joyce M.	*Canonmills and Inverleith*	1994
Wallace, Joyce M.	*Traditions of Trinity and Leith* revised edition	1997
Wilson, James	*Society of Free Fishermen of Newhaven*	1951

RESTALRIG

Cowper, A. S.	*Restalrig Churchyard and Piershill Barracks*	1977
Gray, W. Forbes	*An Edinburgh Miscellany*	1925
Notman, Rev. Robert Black	*Restalrig Parish Church*	1961
Russell, John	*The Story of Leith*	1922
Stirton, E. G. K.	*The Tragedy of Marionville*	1930

STOCKBRIDGE

Environmental Resource Centre	*The Water of Leith Trail: Dean to Stockbridge*	1982
Environmental Resource Centre	*The Water of Leith Trail: Stockbridge to Canonmills*	1982
Hill, Cumberland	*Reminiscences of Stockbridge*	1874
Jamieson, Stanley (editor)	*The Water of Leith*	1984
Kerr, Andrew	*A History of Ann Street*	1982
Magnusson, Magnus	*The Clacken and the Slate*	1974
Pipes, Rose	*The Colonies of Stockbridge*	1984
Pipes, Rose	*Stockbridge: In Living Memory*	1994
Sands, The Hon. Lord	*The Story of St Stephen's Edinburgh*	1927
Smith, John Turnbull	*Sketch of St Bernard's*	1907
Young, George A.	*St Bernard's Parish Church 1823–1973*	1973

Index